BICYCLING
New Hampshire's Seacoast

More Bicycling Books Available from UPNE

Bicycling on Boston's North Shore
by Roger L. Turner

Bicycling Southern New Hampshire
by Linda Chestney

Bicycling with Kids in DownEast Maine:
25 Short, Safe, and Scenic Rides
by Roger L. Turner

Mountain Biking New Hampshire's State Parks and Forests
by Linda Chestney

BICYCLING
New Hampshire's
Seacoast

Revised and Updated

Linda Chestney

UNIVERSITY PRESS OF NEW ENGLAND

Hanover and London

Published by University Press of New England
One Court Street, Lebanon NH 03766
www.upne.com

© 2002 and 2010 by Linda Chestney
Maps © by R. P. Hale.

Originally published by Nicolin Fields Publishing in 2002.
First University Press of New England edition 2010.

The Publisher assumes no liability for accidents happening to, or injuries sustained by, readers who engage in the activities described in this book.

This is an independent guide; no financial support was received from businesses and organizations referred to in the text.

Printed in the United States of America   5   4   3   2   1

University Press of New England is a member of the Green Press Initiative. The paper used in this book meets their minimum requirement for recycled paper.

Library of Congress Control Number 2010921688

ISBN 978-1-58465-871-9

The Library of Congress has cataloged the Nicolin Fields edition as follows:

LIBRARY OF CONGRESS CATALOGING-IN-PUBLICATION DATA

Chestney, Linda, 1952-
Bicycling New Hampshire's seacoast / Linda Chestney.
    p. cm.
ISBN 0-9637077-8-7 (pbk.)
1. Bicycle touring—New Hampshire—Guidebooks. 2. New Hampshire—Guidebooks. 3. Atlantic Coast (N.H.)—Guidebooks. 4. Atlantic Coast (New England)—Guidebooks. I. Title.
GV1045.5.N4 C46 2002
796.6'4'09742—dc21   2002003004

For my fellow pedaler, my "bestest" buddy,
my pearl among the pebbles, my husband, Al Blake.
Truly, the best wine was saved for last.

Bike Rides on
New Hampshire's Seacoast

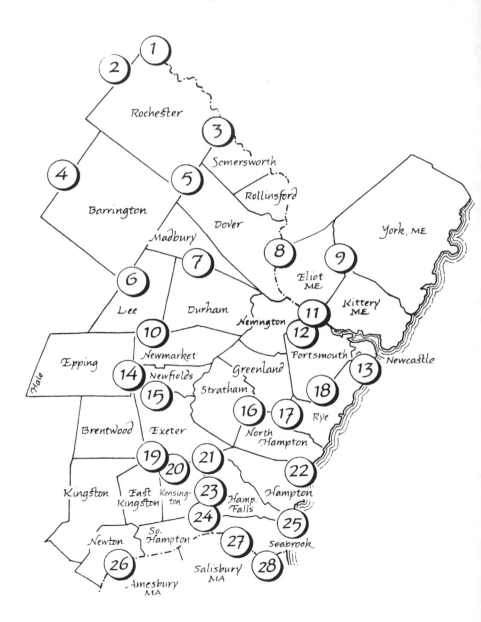

Contents

Acknowledgments

My thanks to the many, many people who helped make this book a reality. A very special thanks to "Baby Doc" Cindy Hoover. I'm grateful for her long-term friendship over many years and many miles!

Thank you to the seasoned Seacoast cyclists who so generously shared their favorite routes for inclusion in this book:

- Thank you to Bee Harvey for the Calef's Country Store (Barrington-Strafford) ride.
- Dolores Rebolledo for the Historic Exeter (Exeter-Kensington) ride.
- Krystina and Tom Arrain for the Lilac City (Rochester-Lebanon, ME), the Jailhouse Tour (Rochester-Somersworth), and the Alton Bay (Rochester-Alton Bay) ride.
- Doug and Cheryl Thompson for their Hodgie's Ice Cream (Newton, NH-Amesbury, MA) ride.
- Nic Orovich for the Inland Seacoast (Newfields-Epping) ride.
- Curt Sayer suggested numerous rides, and among the many, we chose the Massachusetts Farm Country (Seabrook, NH-Amesbury, MA) ride, and the Three Rivers (Dover, NH-Eliot,ME) ride.
- Richard McAteer offered many superb rides. We included a number of them in the book. Among our favorites were: Merrimac River (Hampton, NH-West Newbury, MA), Breakfast Hill (Greenland-North Hampton) ride, and the Nubble Light (Portsmouth, NH-York, ME) ride.
- Barbara Siegert and Joan Drapeau for the Newmarket ride.
- Jim Venne for the Stratham-Rye tour and his valuable work with MS bike rides.
- Cameron Wake for his work on the new bike-ped SABR-bridge included in his Portsmouth-Newington ride.

A special thank you to David Gish for sharing his photography talent on these pages. Classic New England shots—not bad for a California boy!

Although New Hampshire boasts only 18 miles of coastline from Seabrook to Portsmouth, it offers excellent views of the Atlantic Ocean, sandy beaches, and showcases dozens of historic properties and scenic areas.

Introduction

Bicycling
New Hampshire's Seacoast

It doesn't get much better than living on the Seacoast of New Hampshire. New England has a special charm all its own. And New Hampshire is the essense of that New England enchantment.

New Hampshire is its own found paradise. There's a little bit of everything here. Rich history. Classic architecture. Spectacular scenery. Warm people. And lots of backroads that meander through countryside perfect for cycling.

The Seacoast area is particularly blessed with the awesome beauty of the ocean, history that goes back to our country's beginnings, top-notch restaurants, historic homes which are architectural gems, and so much more.

If you're looking for a family activity—a chance for everyone to do something together—to have some fun, stop for a picnic or jump in the old swimming hole, New Hampshire cycling can't be beat. No matter what your age or skill level, male or female, you can find pleasure in cycling. Whether you're a racer or a "let's take 'er easy" rider, you'll find New Hampshire has something to meet your cycling needs. Come on, get out your bike, dust it off and join in the fun of cycling the classic scenery of New Hampshire's Seacoast region!

Uniquely New Hampshire Seacoast

Bicycling New Hampshire's Seacoast is the first guide specifically written for cycling in New Hampshire's Seacoast. For those who live on the Seacoast or those visiting from out-of-state, this book provides ready-made, easy-to-get-to tours.

The rides are designed to keep you off busy roads and introduce you to the serenity of New Hampshire backroads. Occasionally however, a busier road is used because it's unavoidable or designed to take you past a point of interest. All the tours begin at point A, loop around, and bring you back to point A.

A Mole Hill or Mount Everest?

The rides in this book range from 9.7 to 64.2 miles. Most are 20+ miles. They span the gamut from beginner level to more experienced cycling—with the majority of rides in the intermediate range. Some rides are ideal for family riding—choose one with fewer miles.

Bear in mind this *is* New Hampshire, and there *are* hills here. They're unavoidable. If you find a hill too difficult to ride, walk it. Like any other sport, as you get better—the hills get easier—the more you do it.

These rides are for fun! So take a bag lunch or stop at an eatery along the way. Drink in the scenery. Cruise through fragrant apple orchards. Watch the grazing Holstein cattle or the Great Blue Herons fishing. Snap some photos of pristine New England churches. Browse through the antique shops or sit on a park bench and watch the sailboats. Enjoy!

Touring Tips

An exhilarating sport, bicycling can be enjoyed even more when some simple guidelines are observed. With a little common sense, proper equipment, and education, you'll be better prepared to enjoy a safe, fun ride.

Equipment Makes All the Difference

- **Bicycle helmets** save lives. Statistics about head injuries are staggering. A recent five-year study conducted by the Center for Disease Control in Atlanta indicates that nearly three million people suffered from bike accident injuries—and almost 5,000 died—more than half from head injuries. Two of every five head injuries occurred in children under 15. Set a good example—wear a helmet. Make sure the helmet you purchase bears the American National Standard Institute (ANSI) seal or is approved by the Snell Memorial Foundation.

- A **handlebar bag** is a good investment. It holds a lot. Some have a clear plastic map holder to place your ride map and directions in. You can carry tissues, food, wallet, etc., inside your bag. Panniers (saddle bags) are useful for overnight tours or if you make numerous purchases. These two bags mount on a rack over the back or front wheel. If you want to travel very light, snap a fanny pack around your waist. A wedge bag mounted underneath your seat or top tube can hold tools, wallet, spare tube, or a bike lock.

- A **computer odometer** is a necessity. It provides instant feedback on how far you've gone so you can match your odometer mileage to what's noted in the book. Then you'll know when it's time to turn. Your computer may not measure mileage exactly as this book does. Many variables affect its read-out—the amount of pressure in your tires, the size of your tires, how accurately you've calibrated your computer. In any event, the numbers will probably be close enough, along with the landmarks mentioned in the book, so you'll be able to know you're where you should be.

- A **rearview mirror** attached to your bike helmet, sunglasses, or the left side of your handlebars is a smart move. You can then watch traffic approaching from behind.

- Bring a **water bottle or two** with you. Sip water often—even before you're thirsty. Adequate hydration is important for optimal cycling efficiency.

- **Padded gloves** can absorb road shock and protect your hands from potential "road rash" should you take a tumble.

- Many people feel a **gel seat** increases cycling pleasure tenfold. It cushions your rump—undoubtedly a good investment for the "tenderfoot."

More Ideas for a Comfortable Ride

- Remember to carry items such as **tissues, sunscreen, sunglasses** with UV protection, grease clean-up packets (should your chain derail), a spare tube or tube kit, a pump, a basic repair kit, and a first-aid kit.

- To reposition a chain, remove a rear wheel, or do other "dirty work," using inexpensive throw-away (but after you get home!) **latex exam gloves** saves a lot of clean-up time. A pair of gloves will often fit easily in a 35mm film canister, and often only one glove is needed for a job.

- **Bring some cash.** You may want to stop along the way for a bite to eat, ice cream, or a shopping excursion at a yard sale.

- **Food,** such as fresh fruit (cherries, bananas, oranges) or a sandwich, crackers, or energy bars are good for refueling. Snack on something every couple of hours.

- **Dress comfortably.** Lycra clothing is very popular for cycling because it's nice and cool when riding. Its wicking effect absorbs sweat and keeps you cooler than conventional clothing. Lycra shorts are available with padding where it counts—which makes for a more comfortable ride. But if Lycra isn't your thing—no worry—wear whatever is comfortable. But avoid pants with bulky inner seams, like blue jeans or any long-legged slacks which could catch in the chain. Use pant clips (straps) if you *do* wear slacks, or better yet, wear tights.

- A **brightly colored wind breaker** is an excellent way to enhance your visibility. Studies show that neon pink is the most effective because it is not the color of road signs or emergency vehicles and it's the most unexpected color for a motorist to encounter.

- Pick up an inexpensive plastic **rain poncho** that tucks into a packet about four inches square and throw it in your bike bag. New England weather is unpredictable.

Travel Smart Safety Tips

- **It's the law.** Cyclists are governed by the same rules of the road as motorists. And yes, in this state you *can* get a ticket if you disobey the law while on your bike. Follow the same rules as for driving. Ride *with* the traffic. Signal your intentions. Stop at stop signs. Don't ride on the sidewalk.

- Ride **single file**. Ride confidently to communicate to motorists you are a competent cyclist. We need to earn their respect. Too many uneducated riders tarnish the cyclists' image with annoying and unsafe behavior such as riding two abreast or on the wrong side of the road.

- Always carry **identification**—a business card or index card with your name, address, phone number, and information about who to call should you have an accident. Let someone know where you're going.

- The water bottle is also a handy deterrent for nasty **dogs**. Squirting a dog with water will startle it, and often cause it to stop its aggressive behavior. Other suggestions for avoiding **territorial dogs**, try the "holler and point" trick. Shout "Get back there!" or "Go lie down!" They'll often leave you alone. Most bike-dog injuries to cyclists occur because the dog is hit by the bike, or by cyclists losing control swinging a bike pump (or whatever), trying to defend themselves. If the "point and holler" approach doesn't work, get off your bike and position the bike between you and the dog as you walk briskly out of their territory. When there is no challenge of a chase, almost all dogs will become disinterested and go home.

- **Avoid riding in sand**—it can cause a nasty tumble. Be very careful when crossing railroad tracks. Cross them on a perpendicular. Be on the lookout for storm grates. They can cause serious falls. Also use extreme caution on steel-decked bridges and painted surfaces, especially when they are wet.

- **Pace your ride.** Don't take on rides beyond your ability. On long rides, begin slowly. Stop frequently to stretch and walk about. These breaks will prolong your stamina and allow longer, more comfortable rides.

- **Don't use headphones** while you're riding. You'll need total concentration to be aware of traffic hazards.

Join a Club

Cycling is often more enjoyable when it's shared. If you live in New Hampshire, join a touring club. The largest in the state, **Granite State Wheelmen**, is open to anyone interested in bicycling. Organized rides are scheduled nearly every evening in the summer, spring and fall. And for the hardier soul, winter rides are available.

The club also hosts a yearly Tri-State Seacoast Century in September. Yes, that's 100 miles in one day! But you can choose to do 25, 50, or 75 miles instead. It's great fun and you can get a patch that says you really did ride 100 miles!

Different levels of cycling skills are also considered, so you can choose one that's appropriate to your abilities. The club recently added "turtle rides" for the slower-paced, leisure rider. It's fun, and a great way to meet others who love the sport. For membership information, pick up one of their brochures at any bicycle shop or check out their website at www.granitestatewheelmen.org.

The **League of American Bicyclists** is a national organization for bicyclists, formed in 1880. It promotes bicycling for recreation, transportation and fitness, and educates the public on issues concerning safe and effective bicycling. It conducts advocacy work for the full rights of bicyclists. For more information, call (202) 822-1333 or visit www.bikeleague.org.

How to Use This Book

Bicycling New Hampshire's Seacoast indicates the number of miles and a description of the ride at the beginning of each chapter. The number of miles will increase the difficulty just because the more miles you do, the more potential for fatigue to set in.

Evaluate that along with the ride's description (hilly, flat, rolling) and make your decision. Don't forego a ride, however, just because it has some hills. Walking is ok. You're still out there getting exercise and enjoying the scenery. And what better way to impress your friends than to say, "Yeah, I knocked off 27 miles on my bike today."

So get on your bike, shove off, and be prepared to experience the backroads of New Hampshire at their best.

1 *Lilac City Ride*

Rochester, NH–Lebanon, ME

26.5 miles.
Mostly flat, some rolling hills.

Near the Maine border, the quiet, rural community of Rochester, NH, was incorporated in 1722. Back then 60,000 acres of forested land was about all there was to Rochester. Soon immigrants arrived and the complexion of the landscape began to change as farmers carved out homesteads, developed roads, and built mills.

Railroads hit this area in the mid-1800s, and Rochester became the transportation hub of New Hampshire's Seacoast. Traditional manufacturing of products also expanded during this time, producing such items as shoes, woolens, and bricks.

Today, Rochester is a hidden jewel for cyclists. This ride quickly takes you out of town and soon such delightful sights as stone walls, white-paddock fences with horses grazing beyond, old burying grounds, picture-perfect maples, and white colonial churches, will greet you as you skirt into southern Maine.

During the fall foliage season, this ride is particularly enjoyable as the trees change color and present their last-hurrah of dying colors—flaming oranges, brilliant yellows, near-neon reds, and subdued russets. Don't miss it!

RIDE INFORMATION

Highlights: Pretty countryside riding. Nice scenery—horses grazing, maples gracefully overhanging the road, weathered burial grounds, stone walls.

Start: From Home Depot parking lot on Route 11 in Rochester. Take exit 14 off the Spaulding Turnpike. At end of ramp, take right to next stop sign. Take right again. At lights, right into shopping plaza.

RIDE DIRECTIONS

0.0   **Right at lights on Route 11, leaving shopping plaza.**

0.4   **Left on Dewey Street to end.**

0.8   **Cross foot bridge over Cocheco River.**

1.0   **When you see the "Do Not Enter" sign, go right. You are in the Spaulding High School parking lot.**

1.1   **At yield sign, bear right onto road.**

1.3   **At lights, go left on Route 125S.**

1.5   **At lights, go left across railroad crossing on Summer Street (unmarked). Salvation Army is on your right at this turn.**

1.7   **Follow one-way signs to Route 202/11.**

1.8   **Right on Rte. 202/11 (Eastern Avenue).**

3.1   **At light, right on Route 202E.**

3.2   **At light, left on Salmon Falls Road.**

4.7   **Right on Flat Rock Bridge Road.**

5.2   **At stop sign, left on River Road.**

6.6   **Right on North Rochester Road.**

Maples drape this road in all their splendid fall glory (provided you're cycling in the fall, and you *should* be!). Birch interspersed in the landscape add to the serene beauty of the season.

8.2   **At stop sign, left on Shapleigh Road.**

11.3   **At stop sign/T-intersection, right on Center Road (unmarked).**

Faraway mountain vistas, panoramic fall foliage, and picturesque white colonial churches, make this road delightful.

12.5   **Right on Upper Guinea Road.**

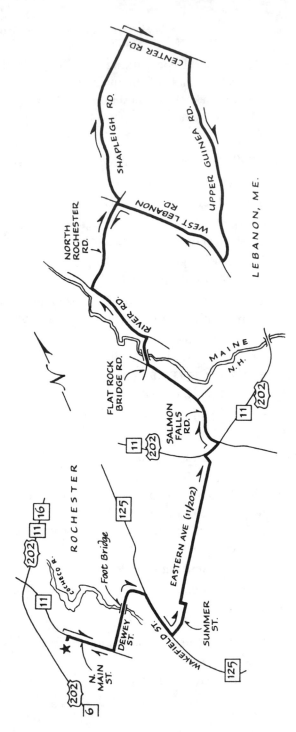

Rochester–Lebanon, ME

16.0   At stop sign/T-intersection, right on West Lebanon Road.

18.3   At stop sign, left on North Rochester Road.

19.9   At stop sign/T-intersection, go left on River Road (unmarked). You are now retracing your steps back to the start of the ride.

21.3   Right on Flat Rock Bridge Road.

21.8   At stop sign, left on Salmon Falls Road (unmarked). This road has fast traffic.

23.2   Right on Route 202 at the light.

23.4   Left on Route 202/11 (Eastern Avenue) to stop sign. Then left half a block to stop sign.

24.8   At stop sign, right on Summer Street.

25.0   Right on Route 125N at lights (by railroad crossing).

25.2   Right on Route 125 at lights (onto Wakefield Street).

25.3   Bear left at yield sign into Spaulding H.S. parking lot.

25.5   Left at the stop sign in the school parking lot.

25.7   Cross the foot bridge, and continue on Dewey Street.

26.0   Right on Main Street (Route 11).

26.5   Left at lights into parking lot of shopping plaza.

2 | *Alton Bay Ride*

Rochester–Alton Bay

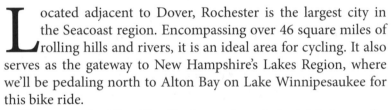

48.7 miles. Lots of hills.
Not a good summer, tourist-season ride.

L ocated adjacent to Dover, Rochester is the largest city in the Seacoast region. Encompassing over 46 square miles of rolling hills and rivers, it is an ideal area for cycling. It also serves as the gateway to New Hampshire's Lakes Region, where we'll be pedaling north to Alton Bay on Lake Winnipesaukee for this bike ride.

Known as the Lilac City, Rochester is an industrial city on the east bank of the Cocheco River. Although granted township in 1623, Rochester's settlement was greatly impeded by Indians. Several later grants were made even after 1656, but the Indian wars kept settlers away.

Rochester dates back to 1722 when it was originally incorporated as Norway Plains. Citizens struggled through rough times and multitudes of Indian attacks. Nonetheless, early settlers brought rich cultural traditions and skills from their homelands.

Farming was the chief occupation with corn and potatoes dominating the farm industry there. Economic vitality was in part effected by the three rivers—the Cocheco, Salmon Falls, and Isinglass. These rivers provided ideal opportunities for farming and industrial growth.

For this ride, we leave the Lilac City and wind our way through pretty backroads and eventually meander along the east side of the Lake Winnipesaukee area known as Loon Cove. The busy tourist town we pedal through is Alton Bay. It's a hopping place during the summer vacation season—so do keep that in mind. The tourist season greatly increases motor traffic.

Enjoy the day, and ride carefully!

RIDE INFORMATION

Highlights: Rock walls, rolling landscape. Horse farms. White paddock fences. A pretty fall ride. (Ride carefully— the Lakes region has lots of traffic then.) Marshlands—keep an eye out for water fowl and turtles. Ice cream stop.

Start: Begin in Rochester at intersection of Old Dover Road and Route 125 at Merchants Plaza.

RIDE DIRECTIONS

0.0   **Go left out of the Merchants Plaza on Route 125S and over a small bridge.**

0.1   **Go right at the lights on Brock Street.**

1.1   **At stop sign/T-intersection, go right on Washington Street (unmarked—a sign here says "Fairgrounds").**

1.6   **Go left on Roy Street.**

1.8   **At T-intersection, go left on Route 202A/Walnut Street (unmarked).**

2.1   **Go right on Twombly Street.**

2.4   **Go left into shopping center (Home Depot here). Go through the shopping center to stop lights.**

2.6   **Go left at lights.**

2.7   **At Y, go left on Ten Rod Road.**

6.9   **Go right at Y on Meeting House Road. (Landmark: Perrault's Auto Body sign).**
     This is a pretty, rolling, curving road.

8.7   **At stop sign, go straight—crossing over Route 11.**

8.8   **Bear left at stop sign on Route 153.**
     You'll soon meander through quaint Farmington Village, birthplace of Vice President Henry Wilson.

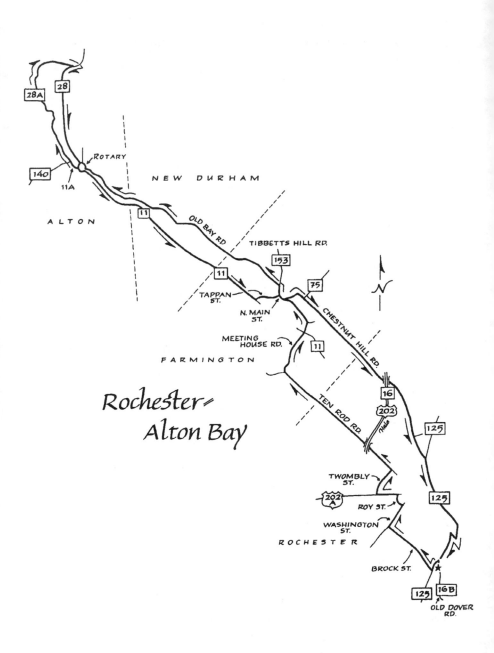

Rochester–
Alton Bay

10.9   **Go left on North Main Street.**
You'll pass by some marshland area. Keep an eye out for wildlife.

14.7   **Stay straight/left at Y on Tibbetts Hill Road—becomes Old Bay Road (unmarked—Ham Road is on the right).**
At about 16.2 miles, Sporto's Ice Cream stand is on the right!

16.3   **Stay left at Y (still on Old Bay Road—still unmarked).**
Soon you enter the small town of New Durham.

19.7   **At stop sign, go right on Route 11.**

19.9   **Go around the rotary on to Route 11W toward Alton Bay.**
This is a busy road, so be careful.
A number of places to eat are located on this road—convenient stores and pizza places.

21.6   **Go right at Y on Route 28A. You'll see Loon Cove on Lake Winnipesaukee on your left.**
At the 24.5 mile mark, expect a long uphill!

25.3   **At stop sign, go right on Route 28S.**
This road has a breakdown lane, and an uphill climb—followed by a nice long downhill!

29.4   **Go around rotary to Route 11E.**

37.9   **Left on Route 75/Tappan Street.**

38.2   **Stop sign at Central Street/Route 75. Continue straight.**

38.6   **At stop sign/T-intersection, go right on Route 153/Main Street.**

38.9   **Turn left on Route 75E.**
A convenience store is located at this turn.

39.7   **Go right on Chestnut Hill Road.**

43.1   **Go right at 4-way stop (Governor's Road on left) on Nute Ridge Road (unmarked).**

46.4   **Go left at "Business District" sign.**

46.7   **At stop light, go right on Route 125.**

47.3   Go left—staying on Route 125S. You're back in Dover. Continue following signs for Route 125S.

48.7   Back at Old Dover Road and Route 125S where you left your car at Merchants Plaza.

3 _Jailhouse Tour_

Rochester–Somersworth

20.7 miles.
Rolling, hilly. Moderately difficult.

R olling through Rochester and Somersworth, this ride offers scenic green meadows, open country roads, and an opportunity to unwind.

Beginning in Rochester, the Lilac City, you quickly blend into the countryside where wide expanses of farmland spread out and with it you feel yourself begin to relax and decompress. Ah, the therapeutic healing powers that nature and recreation provide!

This ride is named the Jailhouse Ride because about halfway into the ride, you pedal past the County Correction Institution complex. A large sprawling network of buildings, it serves a large inmate population.

You also pass through a portion of Somersworth, which offers several natural resource areas including Salmon Falls River, Willand Pond, and Lily Pond—great places to plan a detour from your bike route and have an old-fashioned picnic! Somersworth is also home to General Electric with approximately 600 employees, and additionally boasts the largest Wal-Mart complex in New Hampshire.

RIDE INFORMATION

Highlights: Pretty rolling countryside, corn fields, grazing cows. Ride rolls past the county correction institution.

Start: Begin from Sherwin-Williams parking lot in Rochester. Just off Route 125 on Old Dover Road (behind Merchants Plaza).

RIDE DIRECTIONS

0.0   **Turn right out of the parking lot on Old Dover Road.**

1.6   **Go right on Tebbetts Road.**

2.1   **Go left on Blackwater Road.**
A long uphill on this road. And a nice, long DOWN hill!

5.1   **Go right on Varney Road (unmarked—a house with brick trim is on your left after you turn. If you get to a stop sign, you've gone too far).**

6.0   **Go right on Long Hill Road (unmarked). You'll see the underpass for Spaulding Highway in front of you after you turn.**

7.1   **At stop sign, turn right on Sixth Street.**

David Gish

Ornate fences like this one garner a great deal of attention—almost as much as the stone walls that epitomize classic New England scenes.

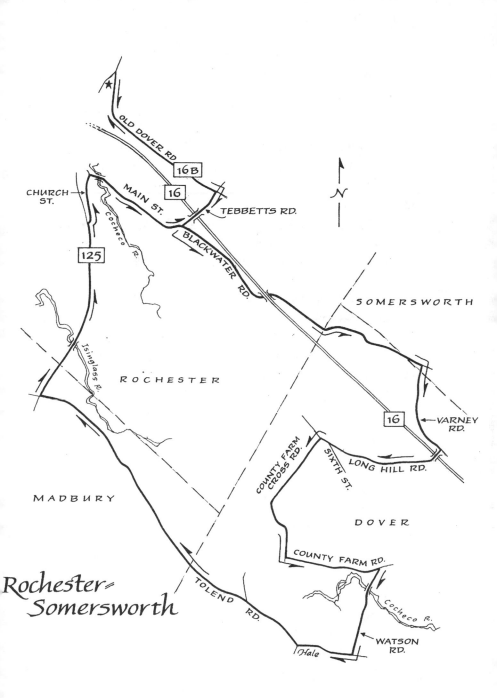

OLD DOVER RD

16B

16

CHURCH
ST.

MAIN ST.

TEBBETTS RD.

N

BLACKWATER RD.

Cocheco R.

125

SOMERSWORTH

Isinglass R.

ROCHESTER

16

VARNEY
RD.

COUNTY FARM
CROSS RD.

SIXTH ST.

LONG HILL RD.

MADBURY

DOVER

COUNTY FARM RD.

Cocheco R.

*Rochester ⸗
Somersworth*

TOLEND RD.

Hale

WATSON
RD.

7.2   Turn left on County Farm Cross Road.

8.6   Go left on County Farm Road.
             On this road is the House of Corrections and other
             institutional buildings. This is a pretty, rolling country
             road.

9.6   Go right on Watson Road.

10.6   At stop sign/T-intersection, turn right on Tolend Road
             (unmarked).

14.9   At stop sign, turn right on Route 125N.

16.9   Go right on Church Street in Gonic, then an immediate
             left on Church Street.

17.4   At stop sign, go right on Main Street by flag pole in Gonic
             Center.
             A pizza place is here on the main street—in case you're
             famished.

18.4   Go left on Tebbetts Road.

19.1   At stop sign/blinking light, go left on Old Dover Road.

20.7   Go left into Sherwin-Williams parking lot.

4 Calef's Country Store

Barrington–Strafford

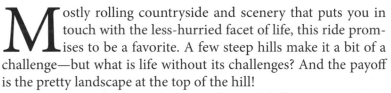

21.3 miles. Not for inexperienced riders.
Hilly, some roads lack breakdown lanes.

Mostly rolling countryside and scenery that puts you in touch with the less-hurried facet of life, this ride promises to be a favorite. A few steep hills make it a bit of a challenge—but what is life without its challenges? And the payoff is the pretty landscape at the top of the hill!

The ride starts across the street from Calef's Country Store. Calef's captures the spirit of the old-fashioned general store with penny candy, a cheese wheel, and a big pickle barrel. Adding to the ambiance, the wide wooden floor boards, worn from decades of use, creak and groan as you walk across them. Step outside and a large covered porch invites one to relax and sit a spell while enjoying a refreshing drink or ice cream cone.

On your bike ride two bridges—one a wooden foot bridge, and another a bridge by a stream with large boulders to perch upon—suggest a stop and perhaps a picnic or a snack break. Do pack a lunch and make a day of it. New Hampshire is too special to be hurried.

RIDE INFORMATION

Highlights: A footbridge for a stop off for a picnic, picturesque Baptist church with stained glass windows, great photo opps, jelly and jam stand, Calef's Country Store, Christmas Dove, scenic cycling at its best.

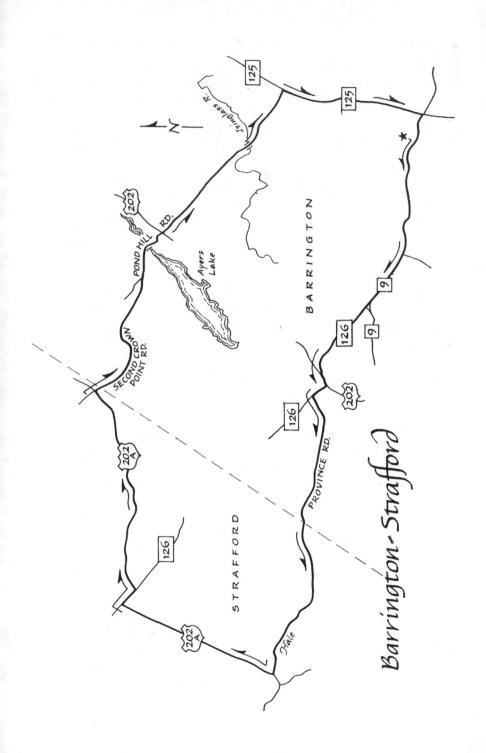

Barrington-Strafford

Burying grounds, rock walls, towering oaks, grazing cows and horses. Classic cliche New Hampshire!

Start: At Route 9 and Route 125 in Barrington, park your car at NH Park & Ride across from Calef's Country Store.

RIDE DIRECTIONS

0.0 **Go right on Route 9 out of the NH Ride & Ride parking lot.**

Calef's Country Store is across the street. Worth a stop. Also after you turn right on Route 9, the Christmas Dove is down the lane on the right. It is a winter wonderland no matter what time of the year it is.

2.7 **At fork, go right on Route 126.**

3.9 **At stop sign, go left on Route 126/202 for a short way.**

4.1 **Right on Route 126.**

4.4 **Left on Province Road.**

You'll begin a steep 0.4 mile uphill climb.

Rock walls, cows, horses, towering oaks, burying grounds, and apple orchards provide pretty scenery along the way.

At 5.7 miles on the left are some strange rock formations. You'll climb gradually for a mile, then a nice, long downhill!

8.6 **At stop sign, go right on Route 202A (unmarked).**

You'll encounter a couple of steep uphills. This road has no breakdown lane.

10.9 **Right on Route 126/202A for a short way.**

11.1 **Stay straight on Route 202A. It curves to left.**

The colonial white Third Baptist Church with its pretty stained glass windows is on this road.

At 12.2 miles on the left is a wooden footbridge—perfect for a break or picnic.

All right—a mile long downhill coming up! Wheee!

14.1   Right on Second Crown Point Road.

Don't miss the photo opp of the hay rake on the left beyond the rock wall with the sun filtering through lacy oak leaves.

15.9   At stop sign, blend right on to Pond Hill Road.

At the 16 mile point on your left, stop for jams and jellies and fill your bike bag. They sell for $2.50 and under. The selection is delicious—cranberry-walnut, strawberry-rhubarb, strawberry-peach, and more. Yummy!

16.7   At stop sign, cross Route 202 to Green Hill Road.

At 18.4 miles a bridge over a wide stream offers an ideal break area—follow the little path down to the stream and sit on the boulders.

19.3   At stop sign, go right on Route 125.

Busy road, wide breakdown lane.

21.2   At stop light, go right on Route 9.

21.3   Right into NH Park & Ride parking lot.

5 | *Rolling Farmland*

Rochester–Dover

15.6 miles. Rolling, a few small hills, one long hill, a good family ride. (Walk bikes up hills that are too difficult for a child.)

Nestled between the Cocheco and Salmon Falls rivers in northeastern Strafford County, Rochester and Dover are close to the beaches, Lakes Region, and the White Mountains. Even though they're off the beaten path, both of these small towns have pockets of congested traffic. The beauty of this ride is that you only skirt the edges of these thriving mini-metropolises.

Known as the "Lilac City" because of the profusion of this fragrant shrub, Rochester was incorporated in 1722 as Norway Plains, later to be called Rochester. In the early 19th century Rochester sprouted factories along the Salmon Falls River, where boots, shoes, woolen goods, bricks, and pottery were produced.

Dover is even older than Rochester. In fact, it's considered to be the oldest permanent settlement in the state, founded in 1623 by fishermen and traders who navigated the waters of the Great Bay area. Eventually the Cocheco Fall's waterpower was harnessed by industries such as grist mills, cotton mills, and saw mills. Today many of the same brick mill buildings that supported the early industries have been renovated, and once again house businesses, but on a smaller scale. The mill buildings blend comfortably with other architectural styles prevalent in the area, especially colonial and Victorian.

From late June to early September, Dover celebrates the Cocheco Arts Festival (603 742-2218). Held in the old mill complex beside

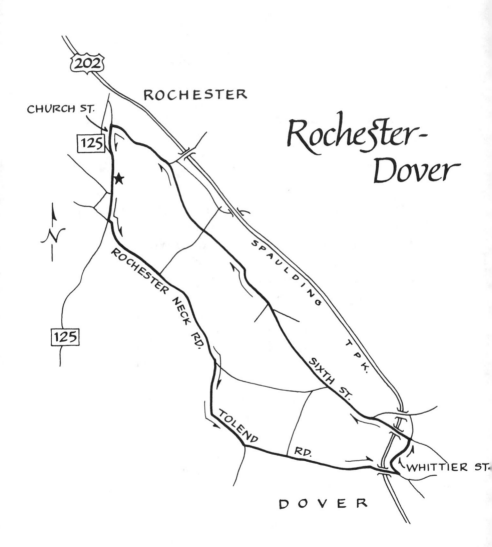

202

ROCHESTER

CHURCH ST.

125

★

Rochester-
Dover

N

125

SPAULDING TPK.

ROCHESTER NECK RD.

SIXTH ST.

TOLEND RD.

WHITTIER ST.

DOVER

the Cocheco River, the festival features children's concerts and programs, as well as concerts for adults by regional performers.

Despite its proximity to Dover and Rochester, this ride is country all the way—and very pretty country, at that. Small cemeteries with granite slab walls. Rolling farmland with hay bales smelling of freshly cut alfalfa. Stone walls. Wild clover and corn waving in the breeze. Now *that's* New Hampshire country!

Bring the kids, a picnic lunch, an adventurous attitude, and have a great day!

RIDE INFORMATION

Highlights: Scenic, rolling farmland. Easy enough for older children—just a little hilly. Minimal traffic, a fairly short ride. Scenic countryside.

Start: Gonic Plaza on Route 125. It's 3.5 miles beyond the Route 9/125 intersection on the left as you're heading north. (At the 9/125 intersection, don't miss Calef's Country Store—it's worth the stop. Great cheeses!)

RIDE DIRECTIONS

0.0 **Right out of Gonic Plaza parking lot on Route 125.**

0.5 **At stop light, left on Rochester Neck Road.**

4.0 **At T-intersection (with a chain-link fence ahead of you), turn left on Tolend Road (unmarked).**

7.3 **Immediately after crossing a bridge, take a sharp left on Whittier Street. Right after you make this turn, you'll see a bus-stop shelter on left.**

For refreshments, Dicicco's Market is at this turn. You'll encounter a steep uphill climb on this road.

7.8 **At stop sign/red blinker, left on Sixth Street.**

This road has little traffic. At 13.7 miles on the right is a Pick-Your-Own Berries farm.

14.6 **Left on Church Street in Gonic. (Just before the post office.)**

If you're starving, Phagin's Restaurant is at this turn.

The small village of Gonic has a pretty, little white-clapboard colonial Baptist church with stained glass windows.

15.1   At stop sign, left on Route 125S.
Caution: storm grates.

15.6   Right to Gonic Plaza.

6 Hot Air Balloon Festival

Lee–Center Barnstead

64.2 miles.
Rolling, hilly, two mile-long hills.

This tour passes through open country with expansive pastures, classic New England barns, houses dating from the 1700s and 1800s, photo-perfect birch stands, and grazing cows and horses. The ride takes in lots of scenery and lots of miles—it's a trip for hardier riders.

The ride begins in the quiet, country town of Lee, then meanders through Madbury, Barrington, Strafford, Barnstead, Pittsfield, Northwood, Nottingham, and back to Lee.

If you plan it just right, you can catch the Pittsfield Rotary Clubs Annual Hot Air Balloon Festival the last weekend in July, where 20+ hot air balloons take flight over the picturesque Suncook Valley. Craft booths, lots of food, entertainment, and an overwhelming supply of town pride are evident at this event.

At about halfway you pedal along deserted roads that lead to Center Barnstead. A cozy, small town, Center Barnstead has its own points of pride—like the pretty Christian Church with colonial appointments, a clock tower, and weather vane. And then there's the gazebo, the weathered war monument on the expansive green, and the well-kept burial grounds.

Those who love antiques will be in their glory on this ride. You travel through Northwood—the mecca of New Hampshire "antiquedom." Whatever you could possibly desire is available—furniture, Depression glass, books, antique shawls and hats, tools—it's all here.

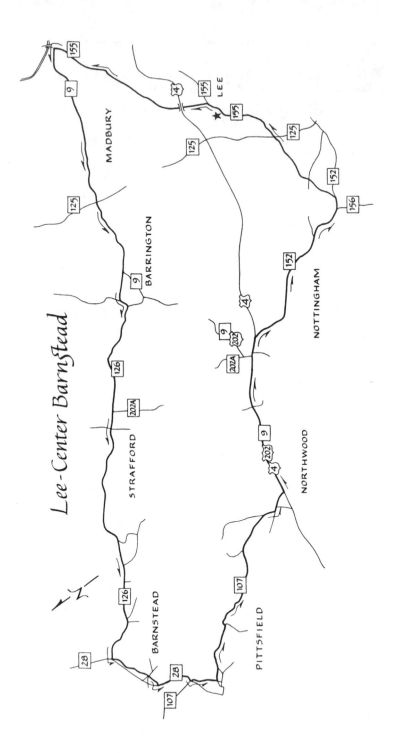

Lee - Center Barnstead

RIDE INFORMATION

Highlights: Historic Calef's Country Store, postcard New England villages, historic buildings, water views, great for fall cycling.

Start: Take Route 125N to Route 155N to Lee center. Park by the Lee Public Library and Lee Police Department.

RIDE DIRECTIONS

0.0 **Left out of the Lee Police Department parking lot on to Route 155N. This road has moderate traffic.**

1.7 **Left still on Route 155N.**

7.9 **At stop light, left on Route 9W.**
This road has a wide shoulder.

14.0 **At stop light at Route 125/9, go straight across—still on Route 9W.**
On your left at this corner is Calef's Country Store. For over a century, they've sold hundreds of gallons of maple syrup, barrels of pickles, and tons of "they'll come for miles around" Cheddar cheese (in a variety of flavors). Calef's was for many years home to the Barrington Post Office and Fire Department. The semi-professional Barrington Orioles used to play baseball in the field out back. The store has seen six generations of the Calef family.

16.8 **At Y, bear right on Route 126N.**
This road has no shoulder and little traffic.

18.1 **At T stop sign, left on Route 126/202W for 0.2 mile.**

18.3 **Right on 126N.**
At 21.2 miles there's a half-mile uphill made bearable by panoramic views at its crest.

22.4 **At stop sign, left on Route 126N. At this turn, directly ahead of you is the Strafford Historical Society.**
The historical society is open by arrangement. Call (603) 269-5461.

Soon on the right is the Military Academy, where the New Hampshire National Guard train. After the Academy, you begin a long, serious climb.

You'll catch panoramic mountain views along Route 126.

Entering Barnstead with its old burial grounds, and white colonial churches with clock towers and bells, you'll have the perfect fodder for a classic New England photo opportunity.

A bit farther brings you to Center Barnstead where the village common sports a gazebo, a war monument, and an opportunity to relax for lunch on the shaded green.

For refreshments, stop at the White Buffalo Trading Post in town. A fascinating old country store, you'll find unexpected pleasures—everything from homemade root beer and assorted candies to antiques and collectibles. Refuel with pizza, a calzone, or something from the deli.

32.4   Just before stop sign/red blinker, turn left toward Barnstead Parade.

34.4   At stop sign, left on Route 28S.

35.3   Right toward Route 107.

36.0   At stop sign, cross Route 28—still on Route 107S.
This is a busy intersection, walk your bike.

36.8   Left in center of Pittsfield, still on Route 107S.
Near this intersection is a supermarket for a food stop.

As you leave Pittsfield, a 1.5-mile uphill challenges you, followed by a steep descent and yet another uphill. (Hey—this is good exercise!)

44.3   Right on Route 107S.

44.9   At stop sign, left on Route 4, a busy road with a wide shoulder. You are entering Northwood.
There are several places along here to eat.

51.5   Right on Route 152E.

57.4   Stay left on Route 152E.

61.0   At stop sign/red blinker at Route 125, cross the road—staying on Route 152E.

62.1   Left on Route 155N.

64.2   Back at Lee Police Station and Town Hall where your ride began.

7 *Horse Farm Ride*

Madbury–Durham

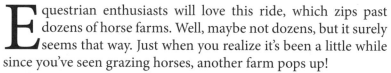

13.3 or 26.2 miles.
Mostly rolling, some gradual hills.

Equestrian enthusiasts will love this ride, which zips past dozens of horse farms. Well, maybe not dozens, but it surely seems that way. Just when you realize it's been a little while since you've seen grazing horses, another farm pops up!

Even if you don't care about horses, you will still love this ride with its curving roads, gradual uphills, big old barns, rock walls, crystal clear ponds, and tree-lined, shaded lanes. And—virtually no traffic! It's a cyclist's paradise!

The ride begins in Madbury, a quiet, rural town of undiscovered beauty that was incorporated in 1768, when about 7,500 acres were carved from western Dover and northern Durham.

Madbury is the only town of that name in the U.S. Part of the reason you see so many horse farms on this ride is that the town has maintained its agricultural roots, with more than half its acreage designated as open space, preserved and protected under Current Use Laws.

Eventually you pedal through Durham, home of the University of New Hampshire, which is the biggest state college with almost 14,000 (11,000 undergraduates) students enrolled. UNH is a competitive school, and admission, even for in-state students, is considered difficult. The campus boasts more than 100 buildings, many of them constructed with such classic architectural touches as pediments, fluted columns with detailed Corinthian caps, and symmetrical facades. Stately brick Georgian and Colonial buildings covered in ivy, dot the sprawling campus.

The UNH Wildcats compete in NCAA Division l-AA and have traditionally fielded strong teams in hockey, basketball, and skiing.

Also located in Durham is an area along the Oyster River known as Durham Landing. Here, in 1694, a force of about 250 Indians, under the French soldier de Villies, killed or captured 100 settlers and destroyed five garrison houses and numerous settlement houses on both sides of the river.

If history interests you, take a side trip to the second floor of the Town Office Building. They house a historical museum at that site.

Hunters beware— these horses come with funeral expenses!

Linda Chestney

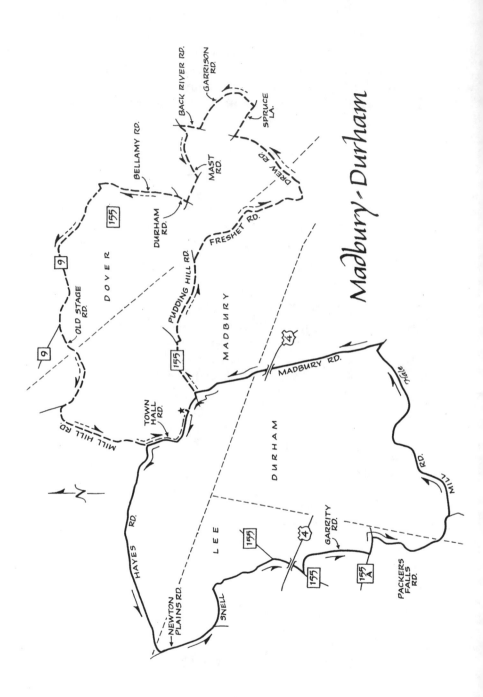

Madbury-Durham

RIDE INFORMATION

Highlights:	A very pretty ride. Many horse farms. Rolling countryside. Rural pedaling past old stone walls, colonial buildings, and a visit to Durham, home of the University of New Hampshire.
Start:	Begin ride at the Madbury Town Hall. It's on Town Hall Road just off Route 155.

RIDE DIRECTIONS

0.0 **Turn right out of Madbury Town Hall parking lot on Town Hall Road.**

The Madbury Town Hall was built in 1861. A simple, white colonial structure with granite steps and foundation, and black shutters, it exemplifies the elegance of simplicity.

0.6 **Go left on Hayes Road.**

Flanked by shady, tall trees, this newly paved road has you pedaling past a thriving horse farm and seemingly miles of wooden fences. The horses graze languidly in the grassy meadows—in contrast to *your* exertion level as you move along this peaceful rolling, winding road.

3.3 **At the stop sign/T-intersection, go left on Newton Plains Road (unmarked).**

4.1 **Go left on Snell Road.**

You'll be challenged by a gradual uphill of 0.4 miles—but hang on—it has a nice downhill on the other side.

5.4 **At the stop sign/blinking light, go right on Route 155 South *under* the overpass.**

5.7 **Go left on Garrity Road. (Don't take Old Garrity Road, it dead ends.)**

6.7 **At stop sign/T-intersection, go left on 155A (unmarked).**

6.9 **Go right on Packers Falls Road.**

Fisher Brook Horse Farm is tucked in the woods along this road. This is a great road—an example of why New Hampshirites love to call this state home!

8.2   Go left on Mill Road.

Mill Road is a quiet, shady, tree-lined road.

10.6   Go right at stop sign in downtown Durham, then a quick left on Madbury Road.

Here in Durham, home of the University of New Hampshire, many ice cream shops, sub shops, and quick food eateries abound.

12.1   At stop light, cross Route 4, still on Madbury Road.

At 12.2 miles at Rose Lawn Farm, you can pick-your-own blueberries! (Email me for a terrific blueberry crisp recipe from the Midwest! nfpi@comcast.net)

13.0   At the stop sign at Route 155, go left, then an immediate right on Town Hall Road.

(NOTE: For a longer ride, don't go left here. See longer ride below.)

13.3   You're back at the Town Hall.

For a longer ride:

At 13.0 miles at the stop sign at Route 155, go *right* on Route 155 North.

13.7   Go right on Pudding Hill Road.

A little climb here keeps you in shape. At 14.2 miles is another horse farm.

14.7   Bear right, now on Freshet Road. (Don't take Garrison Road on the right.)

15.5   At stop sign, cross and continue on Freshet Road.

Another horse farm is along this road. White paddock fences and jumping gates invite you to stop along side the road and watch the show—if you're lucky enough to pass by when they're training the horses.

16.6   Go left on Drew Road.

An old cemetery with weathered stone walls is at this turn.

Also at this turn is yet another horse farm.

17.4	At the stop sign, go left/straight on Back River Road.
17.6	Go right on Spruce Lane (Becomes Garrison Road).
18.0	Road bears left with curve.
19.0	At stop sign/T-intersection, go right on Back River Road.
19.2	Go left on Mast Road.
19.9	At stop sign/T-intersection, go right on Mast Road (unmarked).
20.2	At stop light, go right on Durham Road.
20.4	Turn left on Bellamy Road.
21.4	At stop light, go straight (crossing Route 155) on Route 9W.
	This road's busy road with fast traffic, so ride carefully. A nice breakdown lane eases the stress a bit.
23.1	Go left on Old Stage Road.
	Pretty and tree-lined, this road is a delight to pedal on.
24.3	Go left on Mill Hill Road.
25.6	At the Y, bear left on Town Hall Road.
26.2	Back at Madbury Town Hall on the left.

8 | *Three Rivers Ride*

Dover, NH–Eliot, ME

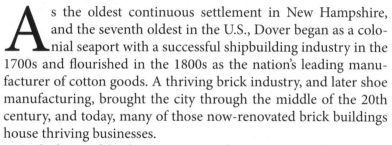

29.4 miles. Lots of rolling hills.
Some challenging. Nice downhills, too!

As the oldest continuous settlement in New Hampshire, and the seventh oldest in the U.S., Dover began as a colonial seaport with a successful shipbuilding industry in the 1700s and flourished in the 1800s as the nation's leading manufacturer of cotton goods. A thriving brick industry, and later shoe manufacturing, brought the city through the middle of the 20th century, and today, many of those now-renovated brick buildings house thriving businesses.

In the heart of the downtown area of Dover—along the Cocheco River—the old mill buildings are undergoing redevelopment and will offer even more commercial space in this thriving Seacoast town.

Salmon Falls River, which you'll cycle past, is southeast of Dover. The Cocheco River cuts through the middle of Dover and empties into Salmon Falls River, which continues on and drains into the Piscataqua River a bit east of Dover.

Another nearby river located west of the Piscataqua River, and paralleling it, is the Bellamy River. It flows south and drains into Little Bay. Coming from a more west-east direction is the Oyster River, which also drains into Little Bay. So this ride is one chocked full of water views.

Eventually the ride meanders up to Eliot, Maine, a rural community situated along the banks of the Piscataqua River. Featuring a relaxed, quiet community, Eliot is home to many tidal estuaries, which add to the pleasure of your ride—hopefully with some wildlife sightings. Enjoy the day!

RIDE INFORMATION

Highlights: Ride has big old barns, winding roads, corn fields, working farms, cows. Open meadows. Stone walls, panoramic views. Swimming beach.

Start: Begin in Dover at Janeto's Market Plaza on Route 108 shortly after the Route 4/9/108 interchange in downtown Dover. Plaza on the right.

RIDE DIRECTIONS

0.0 **Right out of plaza and then right on Broadway at the lights a block up.**

A couple of hills on this road will give you an easy workout. The road has a narrow breakdown lane and moderate traffic.

If you need a bike shop, Dover Cyclery is near where you start—over by Dunkin' Donuts. They're a busy shop with super people to help you out. Check in with them if you need a spare tube or to replace a mirror.

2.0 **Go right on Rollins Road.**

You pedal past working farms on this pretty, rolling country road.

3.8 **At the stop sign/T-intersection, go left (unmarked road).**

A country store is on your right at this corner.

4.9 **At stop sign/blinking light, cross Route/ 4 to Sligo.**

On left is a working farm—complete with a donkey. The Salmon Falls River will appear on the left.
Nice downhill!

5.8 **At Y-intersection by yield sign, go left—still on Sligo (unmarked).**

Cows and donkey graze on the right at this intersection. Expansive, open meadows delight the eye and

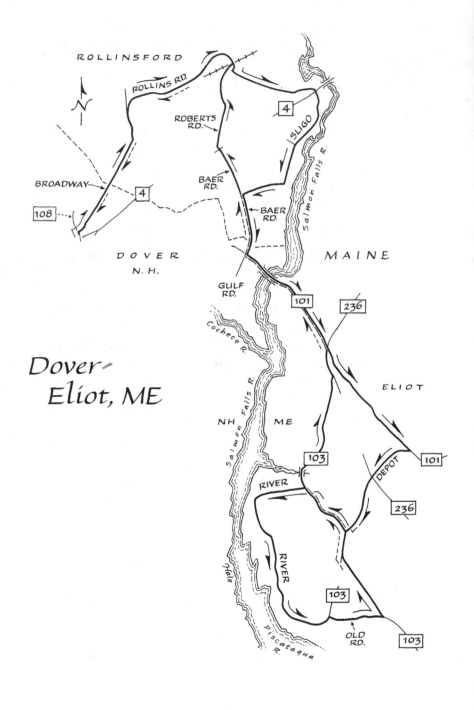

ROLLINSFORD

N

ROLLINS RD.

ROBERTS
RD.

4

SLIGO

Salmon Falls R.

BROADWAY

4

BAER
RD.

108

BAER
RD.

DOVER
N. H.

MAINE

GULF
RD.

101

236

Cocheco R.

ELIOT

Dover-
Eliot, ME

NH   ME

Salmon Falls R.

103

101

DEPOT

RIVER

236

RIVER

Hale

103

103

OLD
RD.

103

Piscataqua
R.

calm the soul. This road deserves "true country road" status with its shade-covered surface and terrific cycling terrain.

You will encounter a steep climb on this stretch. Hey! Stop complaining—hills burn calories!

6.9   At stop sign/T-intersection, go left on Baer Road (unmarked).

Haying the fields occurs in early September. Notice the round bales? It's a modern-day farming method of assuring a well-rounded diet for farm livestock.

This evergreen tree-lined road passes by a horse farm where the large animals graze contentedly in the field with nothing better to do than swish flies away with their tails.

7.7   At stop sign, go left on Gulf Road/Route 101S (in Maine).

This road has no breakdown. At 8.0 miles is the Eliot Bridge, which spans the Salmon Falls River. A swimming beach beckons on the right after the bridge.

9.4   At stop light, continue straight on Route 101S.

Muddy River Marketplace is located at this corner on the right. Stop here for to-die-for baby-back ribs.

At about 10.0 miles on right is Eliot, Maine's version of Stonehenge.

Around the 10.6 mile point, the rolling countryside offers a nice panoramic view off to your right.

11.2 Right on Depot Road.

A nice downhill!

11.8 At stop light go straight—still on Depot Road.

12.6 At stop sign, go right on Route 103.

13.4 Go left on River Road.

To the right along this road is the Piscataqua River. You may catch occasional glimpses of it.

16.4   At the Y-intersection/stop sign, go right on Old Road.

17.1   At stop sign, go left on State Road (unmarked) by library. Same as Route 103W.

20.7   At stop sign, go left on Route 236N.

21.1   At stop light, go left on Route 101.

You'll be backtracking somewhat back to the start. This road has no breakdown.

You'll pass the Eliot Bridge—and the swimming beach—again.

22.8   Go right on Baer Road.

Large evergreens and cottonwoods line this road, and in the fields just beyond the roads, the harvesting of sweet-smelling alfalfa greets your nostrils.

A few hills are sprinkled along this road.

24.4   At stop sign, cross Route 4 to Roberts Road.

A moderate hill challenges you on this road, too. Nice burial grounds along the way will divert your attention, along with the activities of the farm equipment in the middle of haying season.

25.4   Go right at fire station (no street sign), then an immediate left on Rollins Road.

At 25.9 miles: CAUTION! Railroad crossing. Walk your bike. This is a hilly road!

27.3   At stop sign/T-intersection, go left on Goodwin Road (becomes Broadway).

Several uphills give your legs a workout. This is a busy road with a narrow breakdown. Ride carefully.

29.3   At stop light in downtown Dover by Brooks Pharmacy, go left on Route 108 (unmarked), then immediate left again to stop light toward Janetos Market Plaza across the street on your left.

29.4   Back at the plaza.

9 *Nubble Lighthouse*

Portsmouth, NH–York, ME

32.2 miles.
Somewhat hilly. Curving roads.

This is bicycling the New Hampshire Seacoast at its best. The scenery is exquisite. The history is daunting. And the experience is nothing short of exhilarating.

Beginning in historic Portsmouth and hugging your way up the coast to Maine, and eventually to picturesque Nubble Light House in York, this ride promises to be a memorable one. In Portsmouth alone you can find a day full of activities to fill your time. Better yet, take a week!

Portsmouth is the second oldest city in New Hampshire. Settled in 1623 as Strawbery Banke, it was incorporated as Portsmouth in 1631. A major shipbuilding center, Portsmouth prospered and the city has many elegant, historic homes to boast about. If time allows, visit such beauties as the Wentworth Coolidge Mansion (built in 1710), Governor John Langdon House (1784), Warner House (1716), John Paul Jones House (1758), and don't miss the Wentworth Garner House (1760), which was once owned by the Metropolitan Museum of Art and was scheduled to be moved to Central Park in New York City. Fortunately, it is still facing the waterfront on Mechanic Street.

You will pedal through historic Strawbery Banke. Do stop for a tour at the Strawbery Banke Museum, a 10-acre waterfront neighborhood which spotlights one of the nation's first urban sites.

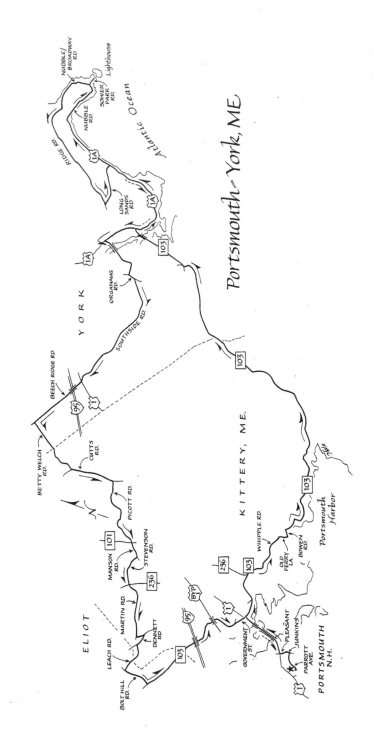

Portsmouth~York, ME

Named by the first settlers in 1630 for the profusion of wild berries found on the shores of the Piscataqua River, Strawbery Banke is rich with history: George Washington, Daniel Webster, John Paul Jones, and John Hancock were all guests here long ago.

Prescott Park, across the street from the Strawbery Banke museum gift shop, is replete with color during the spring and summer, thanks to the dazzling array of thousands of flowers planted there. It's a terrific spot for a picnic or to sit a spell and eat your energy bar.

Today the museum showcases over 400 years of architectural and social change through furnished houses, exhibits, role players, period gardens, traditional crafts, and special programs. Call (603) 433-1100 for hours and additional information.

If time permits, get your hands on a Portsmouth Harbour Trail Walking Tour Guide and Map and indulge in a comprehensive, self-guided walking tour that spotlights the history, character, and charm of one of the most culturally vibrant cities in the country.

Nubble Lighthouse in York, Maine, is one of the most photographed lighthouses in the country.

The tour will take you past tugboats (ripe for a photo opp), historic homes, and magnificent gardens.

Soon you find yourself pedaling through Kittery, Maine's oldest community. Fishing, shipbuilding, and other marine-related industries have been the center of Kittery's economy and history. If you're a shopper, take time to check out more than 100 premiere outlet stores located on Route 1.

Finally you reach York, a gracious, lively community that encompasses 56 square miles of rugged Maine coast. It's also home to Nubble Lighthouse, a renowned landmark that is one of the most photographed lighthouses in the world.

If you're spending the weekend in the area, check out some of the finest restaurants in the state. For terrific Italian food, make reservations at Cafe Mediterraneo on Congress Street in Portsmouth. For funky food and atmosphere, try the Blue Mermaid World Grill "on The Hill," a historic area of Portsmouth behind the Hilton Garden Inn. For the best barbeque house around, seek out Mojo's BBQ on Islington Street. The food can't be beat. There are hundreds more excellent restaurants in and around Portsmouth. Ask other locals for their suggestions!

RIDE INFORMATION

Highlights: Very pretty ride. Wonderful ocean views. Farms. Rolling countryside. Historic Portsmouth. Strawbery Banke. Prescott Park. Nubble Lighthouse. Super restaurants!

Start: Park your car at the Portsmouth Public Library. To get there, head into Portsmouth on Middle Street—shortly before the Islington Street light intersection, turn right—off Middle Street—on Richards Avenue. Just before you turn, a brick, two-story building with columns is in front of you and slightly to your right. Take the first left off Richards Avenue on Parrott Avenue. Half a block up on the left is the library.

RIDE DIRECTIONS

0.0   Turn left out of the parking lot on Parrott Avenue (unmarked).

0.3   At yield sign/T-intersection, go left on Junkins Avenue (unmarked). Then at stop sign/T-intersection, go left on Pleasant Street (unmarked).

0.4   At stop light, go right on Route 1 North/State Street. You'll be crossing the bridge into Kittery, ME. Walk your bike on the sidewalk.

1.2   At stop sign, go right on Government Street.

1.6   At stop light, go straight on Route 103 East. Then follow signs for Route 103 East.

2.0   At stop sign, go right—still on Route 103 East/Whipple Road.

2.8   Go straight (a "right" turn) on Old Ferry Lane.

3.0   At T-intersection, go left on Bowen Road.

3.1   At stop sign, go right on Route 103.

At 4.1 miles is Cap'n Simeons—a terrific place to stop for lunch.

At about 9.3 miles on the left is a jetty where you can take a long stroll. Maybe have a picnic or energy bar break.

9.5   At stop sign/T-intersection, go right on Route 1A North (unmarked).

At around the 10.0-mile mark is York Harbor Inn, an elegant inn to stay at or stop for lunch in the bistro downstairs. They serve a mean hamburger. A park and beautiful views of the water are across the street from the inn.

Soon you enter York, which offers a number of tony places to eat. For a good Italian meal, check out Mimmosa's at about 12.3 miles.

13.0   Right on Nubble Road. Sign here says: Nubble Light.

14.0   **Go right at the Sohier Park loop. Nubble Lighthouse is here.**

Public rest rooms are available. Do take a moment to relax, "shoot" (photograph) the scuba divers, or indulge in some well-earned, yummy ice cream at Fox's Lobster House.

14.2   **At the stop sign/T-intersection, go right on Nubble/Broadway Roads (unmarked).**

Brown's Ice Cream is along this road and is definitely worth a stop! This road offers amazing ocean views. Although, the views are probably even better from the multi-million-dollar homes built along the waterfront!

15.2   **At stop sign, go right on Route 1A North.**

15.6   **At stop sign/T-intersection with a taffy shop in front of you, go left on Route 1A South (unmarked).**

Interesting gift shops dot this street.

15.7   **Turn right on Ridge Road.**

17.7   **At stop sign, go left on Old Post.**

18.7   **At yield sign, go right on Route 1A South. York Historical Society in front of you at this turn.**

18.8   **Left on Lindsay Road.**

19.6   **At stop sign/T-intersection, go left on Organug Road.**

19.7   **Go right on South Side Road.**

This is a fabulous road for cycling. No traffic. Curving. Pretty farm scenery. Buoys hanging from a shed. Picture perfect.

21.7   **At stop sign, stay straight on Beech Ridge Road.**

22.7   **At crossroads by church, go left on Betty Welch Road.**

23.8   **At T-intersection, go left on Cutts Road.**

24.4   **Go right on Picott Road.**

25.5   **At stop sign at Route 101, stay straight on Manson Rd.**

25.8   **Go right on Stevenson Road.**

26.3   At stop light at Route 236 (unmarked busy road), stay straight on Martin Road (unmarked). Martin Road curves to left and becomes Dennett Road Extension.

27.3   At stop sign, go right on Dennett Road.

27.5   At Leach Road (by red fire hydrant), go left.

28.0   At stop sign/T-intersection, go left on Bolt Hill Road (unmarked).

28.2   At T-intersection, go left at stop sign at Route 103, then a right on Pleasant Street.

29.0   At stop sign, go right on Route 103/Main Street.

30.0   At stop sign at Dennett Road, go right on Route 103.

30.5   At Bridge St. stop sign/T-intersection, left on Rte. 103.

30.6   Go straight (right) at fork at Government Street.

30.8   Go right at stop light on Route 1 South. Walk your bike to cross the bridge back into Portsmouth.

31.3   Do a hairpin right turn after the bridge. Road goes *under* the bridge.

31.5   Go left on Marcy Street.
          Strawbery Banke and historic Portsmouth district are along here. Rest rooms at Prescott Park.

31.7   Turn right on Hancock Street.

31.8   At stop sign/T-intersection, go right on Pleasant Street, then an immediate left turn on Edward Street to a stop sign. Go right (on Parrott Avenue, unmarked) a few feet to another stop sign.

31.9   At stop sign at Junkins Avenue (unmarked), go straight on Parrott Avenue. At this intersection, a small pond is across the street and to your left. The brick school building is ahead of you to the right. You'll ride past the school on your right. The parking lot where you started is just beyond the school.

32.2   Turn right into library parking lot.

10 Cattle Ride

Newmarket–Lee or
Newmarket–Durham

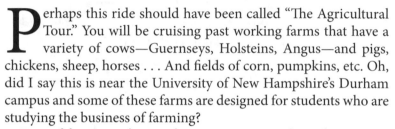

17.9 or 23.9 miles.
Rolling, a few short hills.

Perhaps this ride should have been called "The Agricultural Tour." You will be cruising past working farms that have a variety of cows—Guernseys, Holsteins, Angus—and pigs, chickens, sheep, horses . . . And fields of corn, pumpkins, etc. Oh, did I say this is near the University of New Hampshire's Durham campus and some of these farms are designed for students who are studying the business of farming?

Even if farms aren't your favorite attraction, this ride is a winner because of the relaxing roads you're pedaling on. Tree-lined routes, serene ponds with wildlife, picturesque farm scenes with massive maples in the back yard, stone walls, and rolling meadows, make for a great ride.

You get two tours for the price of one in this chapter. You can choose to go 17.9 miles or 23.9 miles. Both are great rides for the fall foliage season. Lots of hardwood trees to show off New Hampshire's splendid fall wardrobe.

Newmarket is an old mill town which has undergone quite a bit of growth of late, and even the once unattractive old mill buildings are taking on a new face as they're converted into residential condos that sport high ceilings and terrific views of the river. The town is on the Lamprey River, which empties into Great Bay—a natural estuary where fresh and salt water meet. Nearby Moody

Newmarket~Lee ~or~ Newmarket~Durham

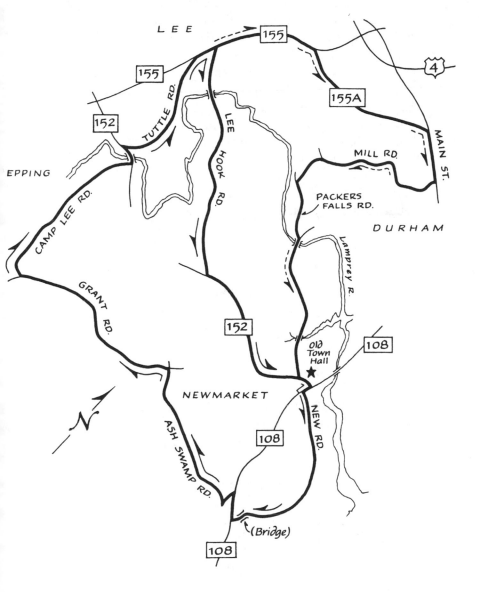

Point offers walking trails, wildlife sightings, docks, and a pavilion perfect for a picnic lunch.

Newmarket is also home to runner Lynn Jennings, U.S. Olympic bronze medalist. Lee is a rural community that offers space to breathe and some wonderful cycling roads.

The extended tour takes you into Durham, where the University of New Hampshire is located, as well as home to the UNH Wildcat hockey teams—both women's and men's teams have impressive wins to their names. The women's team won the national NCAA championship in 1998, and both men's and women's teams were finalists for the 1999 NCAA championship games. UNH's Jason Krog was the recipient of the 1999 Hobey Baker award and he now plays for the NHL.

RIDE INFORMATION

Highlights: Both tours are really pretty rides. Stone walls, working farms, easy pedaling, nice scenery.

Start: Town hall (the big brick building) on Route 152 a block west of Route 108 in Newmarket.

RIDE DIRECTIONS

0.0 **Leave the parking lot on the road perpendicular to the town hall, past Gepetto's Pizza to the intersection of Routes 152 and 108.**

Do stop at Gepetto's Pizza on your return. They have great pizza!

0.1 **At T intersection, go right on Route 108.**

0.2 **Left on New Road.**

This is a pretty, tree-lined road with ponds, and no traffic.

2.6 **At stop sign, turn right on Route 108.**

This is a busy road, but you'll be off it in a jiffy. The Ship to Shore Restaurant at this corner has a varied, reasonably priced menu.

3.0   **Left on Ash Swamp Road. (This is the road across from Great Bay Athletic Club, and to the left of the golf course).**
Tree-lined with stone walls and old graveyards, this road provides pleasant views and no traffic.

5.2   **At four-way stop, go left on Grant Road.**
This is another beautiful road with stone walls, rolling meadows, and an old scenic farm with a massive maple tree and white paddock fences that beg for a Kodak moment.

7.7   **Right on Camp Lee Road.**
Horses graze on a horse farm on this road. More horses laze away summer days at another farm just down the road, where chickens scratch about near the road.

10.0   **At stop sign/T-intersection, go left on Route 152 (unmarked) and cross the bridge.**

10.1   **Right on Tuttle Road.**
Along this road are more horse farms. Also a farm with mud-loving pigs. Pumpkin and sunflower crops arc also harvested here.

11.9   **At yield sign, turn right on Route 155 (unmarked).**

*****

Go to next page for route notes on the 23.9-mile trip.

*****

12.4   **Right on Lee Hook Road (by Jeremiah Smith Grange).**
This road passes one of the UNH agricultural farms. Farms that raise sheep and a variety of cow breeds—Angus, Holstein, Guernseys (Hey—this book is written by a South Dakota farmer's daughter who grew up around cows!)

16.0   **At stop sign/T intersection, turn left on Route 152.**

17.9   **Left into town hall parking lot.**

Directions for the 23.9-mile trip (into Durham):

>   After the turn at the yield sign onto Routes 155 at 11.9 miles, continue on Route 155 through Lee Center.

14.2   **Bear right a bit onto Route 155A.**

16.3   **Right at stop sign on Main Street (unmarked) into Durham.**

>   Numerous eating places abound along Main Street. The Bagelry, Breaking New Grounds, Young's Family Restaurant, pizza places and ice cream stores.

17.5   **Right on Mill Road.**

20.1   **At stop sign T-intersection, go left on Packer's Falls Road (unmarked).**

21.4   **At 3-way stop sign, continue straight on Packer's Falls Road.**

>   If you want to do a bit of antiquing, turn right here and check out Wiswall House Antiques down the road.
>
>   At 21.7 miles don't miss the singing stream where the water tumbles over the rocks creating a mini whitewater area. Nice rocks for a picnic—or wade into the stream and cool off.
>
>   At 22.4 miles a classic old burying ground on your left boasts a stonework wall with horizontal slabs that are so precisely placed, it has endured hundreds of years.

23.8   **At stop sign, turn left on Route 152.**

>   On your right at this corner, don't miss the Deacon Paul Chapman House. Built in 1764, this Federal-style colonial, which features a center chimney, is a fine example of a well-preserved historic structure.

23.9   **Left on Beech Street extension into the town hall parking lot.**

11 Great Bay National Wildlife Refuge

Portsmouth–Newington

14.0 miles.
Mostly flat, a few short hills.

Newington, New Hampshire is probably best known for its malls, Pease International Tradeport, and low taxes. But lesser known facts include that in 1710, the oldest town forest in the United States was established in Newington; that the Newington church bell (a gift from Newington, England) cracked in 1804 and had to be loaded on an oxen-drawn wagon and hauled to Boston where Paul Revere recast the bell; and that it's home to a national treasure—the Great Bay National Wildlife Refuge.

Great Bay National Wildlife Refuge attracts loon, osprey, terns, harriers (marsh hawks), peregrine falcons, and is a winter roosting spot for bald eagles. Common song birds and wild turkeys abound. Coyote, red and gray fox, white-tailed deer, fish, and other mammals are also frequently sighted. This 1,054-acre refuge bordering Pease International Tradeport has a number of hiking/wildlife sighting trails open to the public. To visit, just follow the Great Bay Refuge signs to the visitor center.

And one more lesser-known fact, that we hope remains a secret no longer, is that the new Rockingham Bicycle-Pedestrian Bridge that spans the Spaulding Turnpike connecting Pease International Tradeport to Portsmouth is open! Much work has been done by SABR (Seacoast Area Bicycle Routes), the City of Portsmouth, and the Pease Development Authority to make this a reality. The bridge is finally completed—and this ride takes you there.

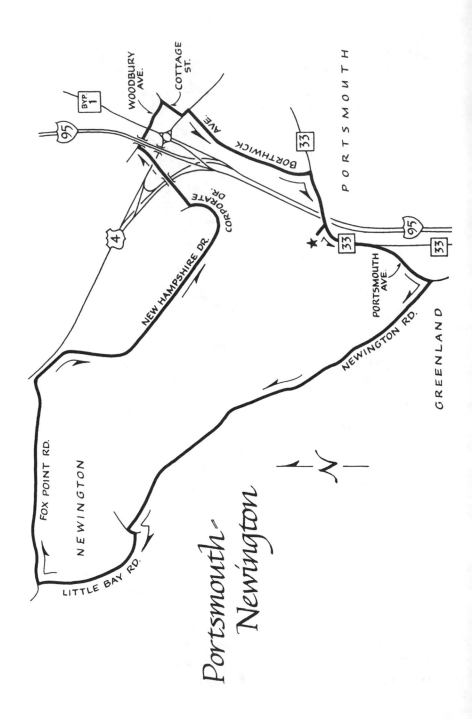

Portsmouth-
Newington

Also consider a side trip to Red Hook Ale Brewery, a micro-brewery located on Pease. Known for its quirky ales and porters, Red Hook is partially owned by Anheuser-Busch. Red Hook offers tours where you can watch the bottling and brewing process, and of course, sample the results. Admission for the hour-long guided tour is $1.

The brewery restaurant is worth a stop also. Food is reasonably priced and quite tasty. They make one mean, tasty burger! Definitely worth the stop!

On this loop ride you will soon forget you're near a major population center as you cruise past apple orchards, cows and horses grazing lazily in nearby fields, lichen-covered stone walls, and ponds teeming with wildlife. Best thing to do is sit back and enjoy the ride.

Keep your eyes open for farm animals. Often they are as entertaining as the wildlife sightings you'll experience on your bike rides.

Linda Chestney

RIDE INFORMATION

Highlights: Rockingham Bicycle–Pedestrian bridge. Great Bay Wildlife Refuge a short side trip. Pleasant scenery. Most of the ride has little auto traffic. Redhook Ale Brewery for lunch or tour.

Start: Bus terminal, and Park & Ride in Portsmouth on Route 33 just west of I-95 access ramps.

RIDE DIRECTIONS

0.0   **Right out of the entrance to the park and ride on Route 33. Start your odometer here.**

0.4   **Right on Portsmouth Avenue (unmarked). Across from Sonoco station.**

1.1   **Right on Newington Road.**

This road offers blooming apple orchards, horses and cows munching in the field, stone walls, corn fields. A relaxing, quiet road.

4.7   **At stop sign, left on Little Bay Road.**

At 5.7 miles don't miss the delightful pine grove and the stately birch interspersed in this forested area.

5.9   **Right on Fox Point Road.**

At 6.0 miles is a quiet pond perfect for a picnic or a photo of ducks and other wildlife.

6.8   **At stop sign cross over Nimble Hill Road to continue on Fox Point Rd.**

7.3   **Straight on Fox Point Road extension. It's a short bike-pedestrian pathway.**

7.5   **Left on Arboretum Drive (unmarked), which becomes New Hampshire Drive, and then curves gent-ly to the left and becomes Corporate Drive.**

You've entered Pease International Tradeport, home to numerous public and private sector organizations, and a focal point in the recovery of the Seacoast's regional economy. Military cutbacks forced Pease

Air Force Base to close in 1991, but its transformation to an international tradeport continues to attract industry.

Take a side trip down Corporate Drive to Red Hook Ale Brewery for a tour—or lunch.

10.7 **Right over bridge—hang on—the "real" bridge is yet to come!**

11.1 **Right on paved pathway with wood railings. The bike-pedestrian bridge appears momentarily.**

11.4 **End of pathway. Take a short right to stop sign.**

11.5 **At stop sign, go right on Woodbury Avenue (unmarked). You will immediately go under a concrete overpass.**

11.9 **Right on Cottage Street to stop light. At stop light, go left one block, then right on Borthwick Avenue.**

Caution! Railroad tracks at 13.3 miles.

13.5 **At stop sign, left to Route 33, then right on Route 33.**

14.0 **Right into entrance of the bus terminal/Park & Ride.**

12 Historic Strawbery Banke

Portsmouth, NH–South Berwick, ME

31.7 miles.
Moderately difficult, hilly.

The second oldest city in the state, Portsmouth has a long history (Dover is the oldest). As far back as 1630, sea-weary travelers disembarked on the west bank of the Piscataqua River to find the ground covered with wild strawberries. The thriving area now known as Portsmouth was originally named Strawbery Banke. Strawbery Banke lives on in Portsmouth's restored historical district, its annual festivals, and colorful Prescott Park—a flower-lover's paradise.

This community initially supported itself by fishing and farming, but eventually turned to ship-building because of the ready supply of lumber and Portsmouth's excellent harbor.

Portsmouth's history is well-preserved in its many old buildings and colonial structures. Wealthy sea captains built finely detailed houses that grace the old cobblestoned sections of town and appear untouched by the passing of centuries. If time permits, take a tour of the Moffatt-Ladd House (1763), John Paul Jones House (1758), Rundlet-May House (1807), Wentworth Coolidge Mansion (1710), Governor John Langdon House (1784), or the Warner House (1716).

Although a relatively small city of 26,000 population, which swells by the thousands in the summer, Portsmouth has much to boast—historic sites and landmarks, Strawbery Banke, whale watch cruises, theater, and outstanding restaurants. Known as the

"Restaurant Capital of New England," the Portsmouth area offers a limitless variety of dining experiences with more than 100 restaurants.

A popular event is the annual Market Square Day held the second weekend in June. The fair features a street fair with 300 exhibits, a road race, concert, historic house tours, and fireworks. Then there's the Jazz Festival, Bow Street Fair, the U.S.S. Albacore submarine, Prescott Park Arts Festival, the Blessing of the Fleet, and more. (Call the Portsmouth Chamber of Commerce at 603 610-5510 for dates and/or information on attractions.)

The bike tour winds along the seacoast for a while, then circles back on less-traveled inland roads through villages in Maine where expansive maples grace the lawns of stately older homes and classic New England churches with towering steeples.

RIDE INFORMATION

Highlights: Historic Seacoast town of Portsmouth, many historic homes, U.S.S. Albacore submarine, Fort McClary State Park for picnicking, historic North Cemetery, fabulous Portsmouth restaurants, great water views.

Start: Memorial Bridge in Portsmouth. Park in Strawbery Banke's free parking lot. (Follow signs down Marcy Street across from Prescott Park). If that lot is full, you'll have to park in the parking garage on Hanover Street. If you have a roof rack, remember to remove your bike before entering the garage.

RIDE DIRECTIONS

0.0 **Start at Memorial Bridge. (Walk your bike.) Cross the bridge on 1N.**

0.6 **At stop sign, turn right on Government Street. Follow Route 103 signs.**

0.9 **At stop light, go straight—on Route 103. Caution: Railroad tracks at about 1.0 mile.**

1.1 **Go right by gas station—still on Route 103E.**

1.4 **At stop sign by gas station, turn right—still on Route 103E.**

> At 3.1 miles is the Fort McClary State Park picnic area on the left. Rest room facilities are available here.
>
> Shortly after the park on the right is Cap'n Simeon's—a yummy seafood restaurant.

8.9 **At stop sign/T-intersection, left on 1-A South in York, Maine.**

> Dignified older homes with expansive maples and historic churches and buildings abound along this road.

10.2 **At stop light, turn left on Route 1S.**

10.6 **Right on Route 91N. Caution: At about 17.7 miles you begin a steep descent with curves, and then a stop sign.**

18.4 **At stop sign, go left on Route 236S.**

21.5 **Right on Route 103E through Eliot, Maine.**

25.8 **Straight on State Road (sign a block up). This road becomes Dennett Street. A gas station will be on your right, and a sign on the left indicates a turn for the post office.**

28.7 **Stay straight for a short stretch on Route 103.**

29.0 **Turn right on Old Post Road to stop sign. At stop sign, go straight across (carefully!) onto Route 1S. (Route 1S loops under the bridge and brings you back up on the other side.) WALK YOUR BIKE ON THE SIDEWALK OVER THE BRIDGE. Riding is prohibited.**

> At about 30.2 miles, a right turn takes you to the U.S.S. Albacore Park and Memory Garden. The vessel served as an experimental prototype for modern submarines. During its service from 1953 to 1972, it tested innovations in sonar, dive brakes, propellers, and controls. A short film is shown daily 9:30–4:00 during the summer. Adults $5.

30.4 **Right on Maplewood Avenue exit to stop sign. Go right— still on Maplewood Avenue. Caution: Railroad tracks at 31.0 miles.**

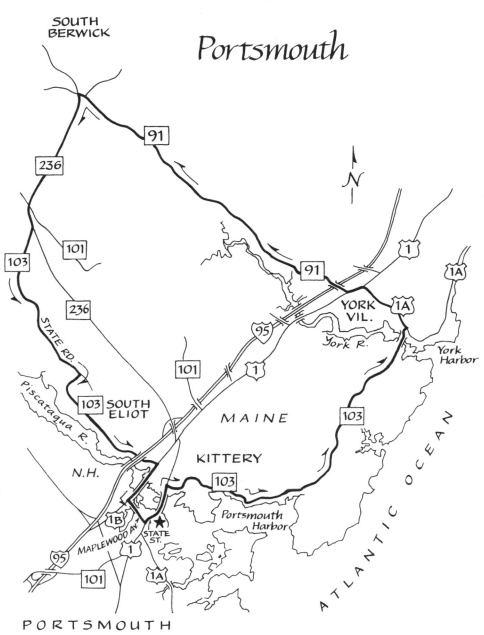

Portsmouth

SOUTH
BERWICK

91

236

101

103

STATE RD.

236

103

Piscataqua R.

103 SOUTH
ELIOT

91

95

101

1

MAINE

N.H.

KITTERY

103

1B

MAPLEWOOD AV.

STATE
ST.

95

1

101

1A

PORTSMOUTH

Portsmouth
Harbor

1

1A

1A

YORK
VIL.

York R.

York
Harbor

ATLANTIC OCEAN

Historic North Cemetery on right at 30.9 miles. Signer of the Declaration of Independence, Governor John Langdon, and signer of the Constitution, Captain Thomas Thompson of the Continental ship *Raleigh*, are among the noted citizens buried here. The cemetery was listed on the National Register in 1978.

31.3   Left on State Street.

31.7   Back at Prescott Park. (Then to wherever you parked your car.)

13 Scenic Ocean and Marsh Tour

Rye–New Castle

22.7 miles.
Mostly flat, a few short hills.

Perhaps this tour should be called, "Scenic Ocean and Marsh Tour." OK. Let's do it! Welcome to the "Scenic Ocean and Marsh Tour." Skirting nine miles of the 18 total miles of ocean shoreline in New Hampshire, this tour also cruises past marshland areas where an abundance of water birds exist—Great Blue Herons, sea gulls, mergansers, loons, and snowy white egrets. Do bring your camera along and capture some of New Hampshire's Seacoast wildlife on film.

Beginning at Odiorne Point State Park in Rye, wending through New Castle, touching a corner of Portsmouth, and back to Rye, the ride will meet your need for your "ocean fix."

While at Odiorne, consider a stop at the Seacoast Science Center. Great for kids, but adults love it too. Explore seven different habitats within this 330-acre park. The ocean, shoreline, tidal pools, meadows, all offer a learning opportunity. Picnic areas, slides and swings, and miles of walking-biking trails enhance the appeal of this park. The park also includes the remains of several pieces of American history—everything from the fishing encampments of the Penacook and Abenaki tribes to the earliest explorations by Giovanni da Verrazano in 1524, to the mysterious-looking camouflaged fortifications built here during WWII. They are strange structures—do plan to ride your bikes around them on the paths.

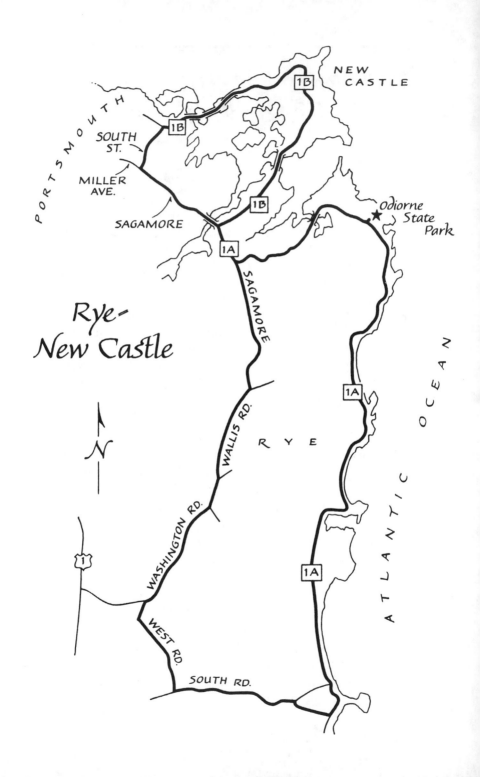

Narrow streets with old houses flush to the curbs lend a colonial air to New Castle, a small village of only 800 people that was originally founded as a fishing village on Great Island in the late 1600s.

President Theodore Roosevelt made history here. He won a Nobel Peace Prize for work done in New Castle—in 1905 he negotiated the Treaty of Portsmouth, which ended the Russo-Japanese War.

Castlelike Wentworth-by-the-Sea Hotel is located on Route 1B in New Castle. The structure was once a haunt for the rich and famous, and was the site of the signing of the Russo-Japanese treaty mentioned above. The building is a gem now that renovations are completed. The grande dame of hotels is a magnificent structure—not to be missed.

The fall is a terrific time to ride this tour, as many hardwood trees line the streets you'll be riding in Rye, New Castle, and Portsmouth. Large maples shade front yards and create lacy canopies as you ride past. Stone walls, grazing horses, and pricey estates also capture your attention along the way.

In historic Rye Center a 200-year-old Congregational church resides along with elegant colonial homes and the newly renovated Rye Public Library.

Cycling along Route 1 (Ocean Boulevard) affords clear views of the Isles of Shoals, a string of small islands 10 miles off Portsmouth Harbor. Most of the islands, which are hardly larger than overgrown boulders, are owned by Maine. The best known, Appledore, is home to a marine lab.

RIDE INFORMATION

Highlights: A beauty of a tour that takes in ocean views, water birds, colonial homes, glimpses of pricey Seacoast estates, and a possible side trip to historic Wentworth-Coolidge Mansion.

Start: Odiorne Point State Park on Route 1A in Rye. Cost during the season is $4 a person; kids 6–11, $2; under 5 free. Park in lot.

RIDE DIRECTIONS

0.0   **Right out of Odiorne entrance on Route 1A north.**

1.8   **At stop sign, continue on Route 1A.**

2.3   **Right on Route 1B north.**
A Great Blue Heron was fishing in the pond on the left after the turn on the day we pedaled past.

3.4   **Caution! Steel-grid draw bridge. Walk your bike.**
At 3.6 miles is Wentworth-by-the-Sea Hotel.

6.7   **At curve to right, go straight on New Castle Avenue.**

6.8   **Left on South Street.**

7.2   **At stop light, go left on Miller Avenue.**
At 7.7 miles, a left on Little Harbor Road will bring you to the Wentworth-Coolidge Mansion, a rambling 42-room structure that overlooks Little Harbor. Considered to be one of the most significant houses of America's colonial era with unusual architecture from 1690–95, it was the official Royal Governor's residence.

8.2   **Caution! Another steel-grid bridge. Walk your bike.**

8.9   **Right on Sagamore by gas station.**

10.4   **At stop sign by gas station, go right on Wallis Road (unmarked).**
At 11.2 miles on the right, surrounded by a picket fence, is a colonial cape built in 1765, the Joseph Rand house. Note the field stone foundation.

For antique lovers, stop in at Antiques at Rye on your right at 11.4 miles.

Some multi-million dollar, palatial homes line this street as you follow it out to the ocean.

11.5   **Stay straight on this road by the junior high school. You'll now be on Washington Road.**
Soon you'll pass through historic Rye Center—and past the white colonial church and town hall.

11.9   **At Y-intersection by the church, stay straight, to continue on Washington Road (unmarked).**

13.3   **Left on West Road.**

Christine's Crossing is located at this turn—a unique store with unusual clothing and accessories. Worth stopping in.

14.5   **Left on South Road.**

16.0   **At Y and stop sign, bear left—still on South Road, and follow it to the ocean.**

16.4   **Left on Route 1A (Ocean Boulevard). The ocean!**

There are numerous places to stop and grab a bite to eat or an ice cream cone along Route 1A.

Jennis Beach has rest rooms.

22.7   **Right into Odiorne State Park.**

14 *Inland Seacoast Ride*

Newfields–Epping

*29.1 miles over paved roads
or 30.7 miles including off-road stretches.
Rolling, a few moderate hills.*

Newfields, a bedroom community for commuters to Boston, Portsmouth, and Manchester, is a lovely rural town that is proud of its lack of traffic lights (there's only one) and the lack of traffic congestion that goes with it.

It's the perfect small town to begin a leisurely bike ride. Newfields Center has a couple of pretty white New England churches, a town municipal area, and numerous rambling old homes that seem to say, "Stop and relax awhile."

You have two options for the beginning of this ride—Start 1 from Newfields Town Hall for an all "on-road" ride or Start 2 from the old Newfields train station, which includes an "off-road" experience on the eastern end of the Rockingham Recreation Trail (also known as the Rockingham Rail Trail). Both rides continue on the same roads after they converge about 3.5 miles from the start. The starting points are 1.5 miles apart.

All across the country unused railroad corridors have been converted into public, multi-use trails. This one is a gem. The Rockingham Rec trail is a roughly 54-mile-long triangle that has three distinct legs—with "points of the triangle" in Newfields/Epping, Manchester/Auburn, and Windham. We only take you on a small stretch of the trail, but feel free to follow it as far as you'd like! (If you want the complete trail map and information, check out my book, *Mountain Biking New Hampshire's State Parks and Forests* or visit www.traillink.com/ViewTrail.aspx?AcctID=6031848. The trail is best navigated with a hybrid or mountain bike, because occasional stretches of stones and sand don't lend themselves to skinny tires.

From Newfields we travel into the old mill town of Newmarket, then through the college town of Durham, up through Lee, Epping, blend briefly into Fremont, Brentwood, Exeter, and back to Newfields.

This ride offers little in the way of tourist attractions or historic sites, but is still pretty country riding at its best!

RIDE INFORMATION

Highlights: Rock walls. Horse farms. For the photographically inclined, lots of photo opportunities. Old colonial homes. Weathered stone walls. A perfect fall ride. A great summer ride, too, as most of the route is well shaded.

Start 1: This 29.1-mile route is all on roads. Begin at Newfields' Town Hall on Route 85, Newfields' Main Street. They have a huge parking lot.

Start 2: This 30.7-mile route has a 3.3 mile off-road stretch at the beginning and end (if you return the same way). For the rail-trail ride (hybrid bicycle recommended), start at the rail-trailhead in Newfields. From stop light at Routes 108/85, head north on 108, cross the active rail line, take first left on Ash Swamp Road. Go straight to the end of the road and park your car to the right of the old train depot. Rail trail is to your right.

RIDE DIRECTIONS

Start 1

0.0 **Turn left out of the town hall parking lot and head south on Route 85.**

0.2 **Turn right on Route 87, Piscassic Road.**
(Then follow directions below from 3.5 miles.)

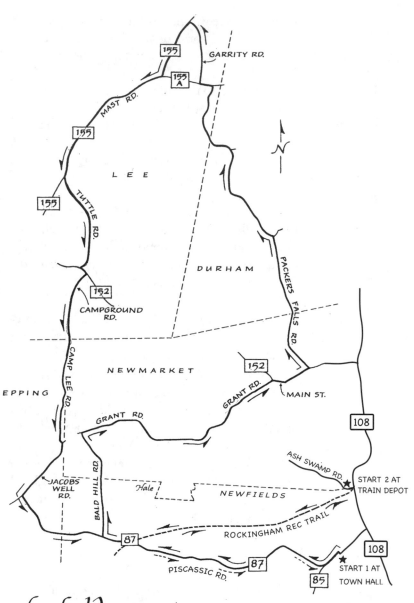

155

GARRITY RD.

155
A

MAST RD.

155

L E E

155

TUTTLE RD.

152

CAMPGROUND RD.

DURHAM

PACKERS FALLS RD.

CAMP LEE RD.

N E W M A R K E T

152

GRANT RD.

MAIN ST.

EPPING

108

GRANT RD.

JACOBS WELL RD.

BALD HILL RD.

Hale

ASH SWAMP RD.

NEWFIELDS

★ START 2 AT TRAIN DEPOT

87

ROCKINGHAM REC TRAIL

87

108

PISCASSIC RD.

85

★ START 1 AT TOWN HALL

Newfields = Epping

Start 2

0.0 **Head down rail trail for 3.3 miles—crossing two streets along the way. At the third street (unmarked, but it's Route 87/Piscassic Road), turn right on Route 87 for 0.2 miles. Then follow directions below at 3.5 miles.**

The rail trail portion of this route passes through an interesting wetland, and is wonderfully shaded and cool on a hot summer day.

Both rides continue:

3.5 **Turn right (by cemetery) on Bald Hill Road.**

Wonderful old burial grounds are at this turn. This cemetery with its rock wall, wrought-iron fence, massive maple trees, and interesting headstones, is a terrific photo opp.

5.2 **At stop sign/Y-intersection, turn right on Grant Road.**

7.4 **At stop sign, continue straight—still on Grant Road.**

8.6 **At stop sign/T-intersection at Wadleigh Falls Road, go right on Main Street in Newmarket.**

9.2 **Go left on Packers Falls Road.**

At this corner, notice the historic Deacon Paul Chapman House with the center chimney. Built in 1764, this Federal-style colonial is a fine example of a well-preserved historic structure.

At 11.2 miles a pretty bridge invites you to sit upon the large boulders and enjoy a picnic lunch.

Also along this road reside three old, weathered burying grounds, beautiful spreading maple trees, and a granite block wall built in the middle 1800s.

11.6 **At stop sign, stay straight—still on Packers Falls Road.**

12.2 **Stay right with curve in the road—still on Packers Falls Road. (Sign says: Wednesday Hill Road—but Wednesday Hill is the road going straight—you want to follow the curve to the right.)**

14.1 **At stop sign/T-intersection, go left on Route 155A (unmarked).**

14.3   Turn right on Garrity Road.

This tree-lined road dances with leaves during fall foliage season.

15.3   At stop sign/T-intersection, go left on Route 155/Turtle Pond Road (unmarked).

16.2   At stop sign/T-intersection go right on 155 South/Mast Road.

18.5   Left on Tuttle Road.

20.3   At stop sign, take a left on Route 152, cross the bridge, then take an immediate right on Campground Road. (Becomes Camp Lee Road.)

Before you turn left, notice the farm on your right, which sports a breathtaking maple tree—especially gorgeous during foliage season. Worth a shot!

22.5   At stop sign/T-intersection, turn right on Jacobs Well Road.

Deer have been sighted on this road early mornings. If you're riding then, keep an eye out!

23.8   At stop sign/T-intersection, turn left on Route 87 (unmarked). If you'd like to finish the ride on the rail trail, travel 1.8 miles after this turn, then go left on the rail trail (which is shortly after a cemetery on your left).

28.8   At stop sign/T-intersection, go left on Route 85.

29.1   Back at town hall on your right in Newfields Center.

End of on-road ride.

To return to your car at Start 2, the old railroad depot, continue on Route 85 (past the town hall on your right) another 0.6 miles to the stop lights.

29.7   At stop light, go left on Route 108.

Be careful here. Traffic can be fast. You'll be on this road only a short while.

30.5   Turn left on Ash Swamp Road. Go straight through a small intersection.

30.7   You're back at the abandoned railroad depot.

15 Durham Point

37.4 miles.
Rolling, with lots of moderate hills.

E xeter and Durham. These two small Seacoast towns are known for their academic institutions—Exeter for Phillips Exeter Academy and Durham for the University of New Hampshire.

Exeter, a 350-year-old New England community, is home to one of the most famous preparatory schools in the country—Phillips Exeter Academy, founded in 1783. The sprawling campus with its ivy-covered brick buildings is located in the Front Street Historic District. Here architectural design spans the gamut from historic colonial homes constructed in the 1600s and 1700s—like the Gilman Garrison House (1690) and Cincinnati Memorial Hall (1721)—to the contemporary Phillips Exeter Academy Library designed by Louis Kahn.

If you have the time and inclination, plan to take a historic walking tour of Exeter. Booklets for four self-guided tours are available from the Exeter Area Chamber of Commerce at 120 Water Street. Guided tours are also offered by the American Independence Museum, One Governors Lane.

Exeter also offers unique specialty shops—a card shop with over 3,000 cards, a collector's book store, a toy store with prices from $10 to $300. Exeter boasts some of the best restaurants around. The cuisine ranges from down-homesy casual restaurants with steaming chowders and home-baked "Annadamma" bread, to Szechuan and international gourmet elegance.

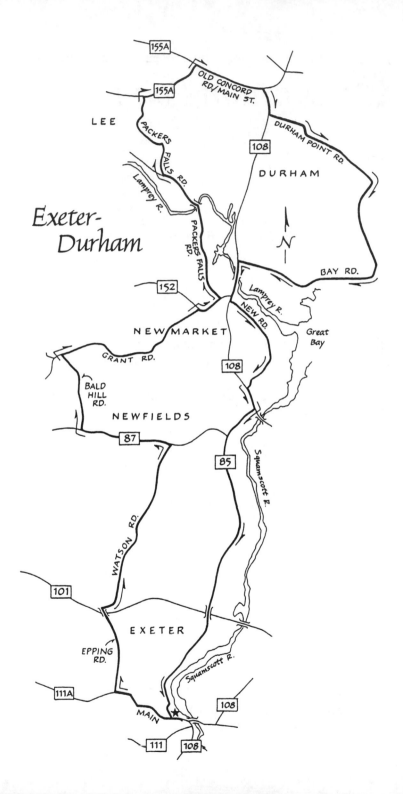

Halfway through your ride, you enter Durham. Durham ranks among New Hampshire's oldest towns. In its colonial days, Durham was the scene of some of the worst Indian massacres in American history. Today, a calmer atmosphere prevails in this collegiate town, which harbors 14,000 University of New Hampshire students.

RIDE INFORMATION

Highlights: Several historic markers, Arabian horse farms, numerous well-kept burying grounds, a couple choice picnic spots, historic houses and walking tours, classic colonial architecture, Phillips Exeter Academy, the University of New Hampshire, and an apple orchard.

Start: In downtown Exeter park in the municipal parking lot on Water Street (the main street) by Szechuan Taste.

RIDE DIRECTIONS

0.0 **Left out of parking lot on Water Street/Main Street. (This becomes Epping Road, and is also Route 27W). Caution: Railroad tracks at 0.6 mile. Stay on Route 27W to cross over Route 101.**

2.5 **Right on Watson Road. Becomes Oakland Road.**

5.2 **At stop sign/T-intersection, go left on Route 87 (unmarked).**

On this road you pedal past towering silos, a prosperous horse farm, majestic maples, and a stately, Federal-style colonial home built in 1740.

7.2 **Right on Bald Hill Road.**

This turn is by old burying grounds, dignified with expansive maples gracing its stone wall.

8.9 **At stop sign/Y-intersection, go right on Grant Road.**

11.2 **At stop sign, go straight—still on Grant Road.**

There's an Arabian Horse Farm on this road.

12.4 **At stop sign, go right on Route 152E.**

12.9   Left on Packer's Falls Road.

At this turn, don't miss the historic Deacon Paul Chapman House. Built in 1764, this Federal-style colonial features a center chimney, and is a fine example of a well-preserved historic structure.

At about 15.0 miles a bridge crosses over rushing water. Flat boulders invite you to stop and have a picnic. Also this road boasts three old, weathered burying grounds, spreading maple trees, and a granite block wall built in the mid-1800s.

15.3   At stop sign, stay straight. Wiswall Road on left.

16.0   Bear right with the curve.

17.9   Stop sign. Go right on Route 155A (unmarked).

19.2   At stop sign, turn right on Main Street (unmarked) through Durham.

Along Durham's main street, many eateries offer a chance to grab a bite or indulge in ice cream!

20.7   Right on Route 108S. Caution: Busy intersection!

This turn takes you past the colonial Community Church of Durham. The cupola dates back to circa 1849.

Also along this road are several historic markers. Major General John Sullivan (1740–1795), a revolutionary patriot, soldier and politician, served under Washington from Cambridge to Valley Forge. Later he served three terms as governor of New Hampshire.

The Oyster River Massacre and the Packer's Falls historic marker are also here. The falls, a couple of miles from this point on the Lamprey River, once provided waterpower and industry for early settlers.

21.1   Left on Durham Point Road. Becomes Bay Road.

This is a hilly, but outrageously wonderful stretch of road with fabulous views of Great Bay, occasional glimpses of Great Blue Herons fishing in the marshes, and terrific fall riding! Note at 23.7 miles on the right is an 1834 brick school house.

28.9 **At stop sign, left on Route 108S (unmarked) through Newmarket.**

Soon you pass a cluster of mill buildings in the industrial area of Newmarket, and places to eat.

29.2 **Bear left, staying on Route 108S. Caution: busy road.**

29.5 **Left on New Road.**

This is a pretty, tree-lined road with ponds and no traffic.

31.9 **Left on Route 108S a short way.**

32.3 **Right on Route 85S through Newfields, and back to Exeter. Caution: Lots of traffic.**

This stretch of road has two architecturally noteworthy New England churches with such classic architectural features as Gothic stained glass windows, rose windows, and bell towers.

Newfields Country Store is on this road for food.

A historic marker along this road notes the life of Brigadier General Enoch Poor. A successful merchant and ship builder, Poor served under Washington, Sullivan, and Lafayette. Congress commissioned him Brigadier General in 1777.

33.7 **At Y, bear left through Swasey Parkway.**

This is a pretty place for a picnic—complete with a mesmerizing, gentle waterfall.

37.2 **At stop sign, turn left on Main Street (Water Street).**

37.4 **You're back at the municipal parking lot (on the right) where your ride began.**

16 Historic Rye

Stratham–Rye

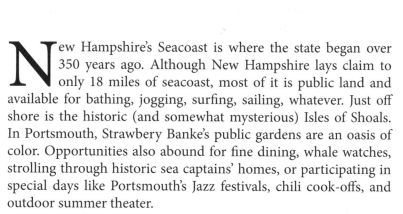

26.3 miles.
Mostly flat, a few short hills.

New Hampshire's Seacoast is where the state began over 350 years ago. Although New Hampshire lays claim to only 18 miles of seacoast, most of it is public land and available for bathing, jogging, surfing, sailing, whatever. Just off shore is the historic (and somewhat mysterious) Isles of Shoals. In Portsmouth, Strawbery Banke's public gardens are an oasis of color. Opportunities also abound for fine dining, whale watches, strolling through historic sea captains' homes, or participating in special days like Portsmouth's Jazz festivals, chili cook-offs, and outdoor summer theater.

Cruising through the quiet bedroom communities of Stratham, North Hampton, and Rye, this ride offers excellent scenery and some unexpected surprises. For example, as you pedal along the swamp land on Lovering Road in North Hampton, which parallels nearby I-95, who would think that wildlife would flourish so close to a busy thoroughfare? But it does. Early in the morning you can sometimes observe elusive deer grazing in the field, painted turtles sunning on rocks, and of course in early spring, red-winged black birds darting among marsh reeds.

Continuing on the ride, you'll soon encounter the spark-ling ocean in all its majesty. In Rye you cycle through the historic vil-lage center. A 200-year-old Congregational church resides here along with historic colonial homes, and the renovated Rye Public Library.

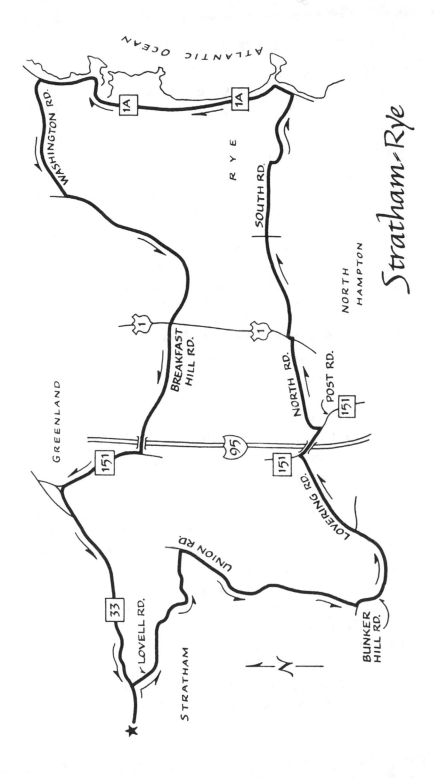

A bit busier traffic-wise than most rides in this book, this tour is nevertheless worth the effort. A popular tourist destination, the Seacoast of New Hampshire is a jewel worth adding to your treasure trove of experiences. Enjoy the ride.

RIDE INFORMATION

Highlights: A beauty of a tour that takes in ocean views, rural roads, glimpses of pricey Seacoast estates, and quite possibly wildlife sightings.

Start: Stratham Hill Park is 1.9 miles east of the Stratham Circle on Route 33E, on right.

RIDE DIRECTIONS

0.0   **Right out of the park on Route 33E.**

A very busy, fast-trafficked road, but with a nice breakdown lane. You won't be on it long.

The park has picnic tables and a covered pavilion, so bring a picnic lunch!

0.6   **Right on Lovell Road.**

1.4   **Right on Willow Brook Avenue.**

1.9   **At stop sign/T-intersection, left on High Street.**

2.6   **Right on Union Road.**

3.8   **At stop sign continue straight, still on Union Road.**

At 4.5 miles, animal lovers note Rolling Meadow Pet Cemetery on the left. This pet resting place is managed by NHSPCA in Stratham, a wonderful organization for matching animals with owners.

5.0   **Left on Bunker Hill Road.**

6.0   **At stop sign, go straight on Lovering Road.**

Marshes along this road are teeming with turtles, frogs, and ducks. Deer have also been sighted.

7.5   **Right on Post Road (Route 151S). Cross over I-95.**

7.8   **Left on North Road.**

9.1   **Left on Route 1. This is a very busy road. Be careful! (But you'll only be on it for 0.1 of a mile.)**

9.2   **Right on North Road (continuing). North Road becomes South Road when you cross into Rye.**

Some multi-million dollar, palatial homes line this street as you follow it out to the ocean.

11.9   **At stop sign, continue straight on South Road.**

12.4   **Left on Route 1A (Ocean Boulevard). The ocean!**

There are numerous places to stop and grab a bite to eat or an ice cream cone along Route 1A.

At 13.0 miles, Jennis Beach has rest rooms.

15.5   **Left on Washington Road.**

17.0   **Bear left at stop sign to continue on Washington Road. (Rye Junior High will be on your right.)**

Soon you'll be in the historic center of Rye—by the white colonial church and town hall.

17.4   **Stay straight at fork, continue on Washington Road.**

At 18.6 miles, a convenience store is on your right.

Buoys dot the Seacoast area of New Hampshire—on land and on sea. Each fisherman has buoys with distinctive colors to differentiate them from others in the same fishing locale.

Linda Chestney

19.6   **Cross Route 1 to Breakfast Hill Road.**

21.3   **At stop sign, go right on Route 151.**

22.4   **Stay right, still on Route 151 to light.**
             For super pizza and subs, stop at the Greek-owned
             Greenland House of Pizza on your right at 22.6 miles,
             or Mizuna's Market & Café for terrific deli sandwiches
             on the right at Route 151.

22.8   **At the stop light, turn left on Route 33.**
             This road has fast traffic.

26.3   **Left at Stratham Hill Park.**

17 *Breakfast Hill*

Greenland–North Hampton

16.5 or 20.0 miles.
Relatively flat, with a few short hills.

B reakfast Hill. If you live on the Seacoast of New Hampshire, you *might* know where the name comes from. Although I've lived on the Seacoast for 15 years, I still could find no one to answer the question, "Where did 'Breakfast Hill' come from?"—until I connected with Paul Hughes.

He is Greenland's resident historian, and in fact has just completed a book on the history of Greenland. He explains that the name comes from a raid on colonists by Maine Indians in June of 1696. They had stolen ashore near Sandy Beach in Rye, attacked and burned five houses, killed 14 of the occupants, and then took four captives.

The next morning the Portsmouth militia, in diligent pursuit, discovered the Indians as they were cooking breakfast on the hill across the road from where Bethany Church is now located in Greenland on Breakfast Hill Road.

A surprise attack interrupted their meal. The captives were freed and the Indians chased back to the sea shore, where they climbed in their canoes and paddled away. Hence, the location bears the name Breakfast Hill to this day.

This bike ride begins on Breakfast Hill in Greenland, and travels through sneaky backroads of Seacoast communities—roads often frequented by the locals as they navigate to avoid the traffic during the tourist seasons.

After leaving Greenland, you travel through historic Rye, where Captain John Smith settled in 1614. He considered the area an earthly paradise. This historic fishing village encompasses eight of New Hampshire's 18 miles of coastline, as well as three of the Isles of Shoals—Star Island, White Island Lighthouse, and Lunging Island—located six miles offshore. (To glimpse these islands, check out the Rye-Portsmouth ride.)

Soon you blend into North Hampton. Along the way, you pass the Little River Cemetery. Poet Ogden Nash is laid to rest here, as is Massachusetts Governor Alvan T. Fuller, and veterans of many wars. One gravestone that many find curious is the Batchelder family memorial, which is capped with the figure of a reclining dog. During the Victorian era, animals, such as a dog or more commonly a lamb, were used to mark the graves of children.

As you continue through North Hampton, you enter the North Hill area of North Hampton, where the town green and gazebo reside. The Congregational Church was built in 1838. To the left of the church and across from the green is Centennial Hall. In 1876, John Hobbs built this structure for $11,000 as a gift to the town

Linda Chestney

During the Victorian era, animals, such as a dog or more commonly a lamb, were used to mark the graves of children.

when its growing population needed more school space. Later turned over to the town, the Friends of Centennial Hall, a non-profit organization, is currently restoring the building as a creative and performing arts center.

RIDE INFORMATION

Highlights: Although not along the ocean, this is still a very pretty ride. This ride is more inland to show you some lesser-known areas of the Seacoast, historic Rye Center and North Hampton, sprawling horse farms, stately Victorian and colonial homes.

Start: Begin at Bethany Church parking lot in Greenland. The church is located on Breakfast Hill Road, which is a turn off Route 1 in Rye—at the intersection of Washington Road and Breakfast Hill Road. Look for the tall white spire.

RIDE DIRECTIONS

0.0 **Turn right out of parking lot on Breakfast Hill Road. (Use exit nearest Route 1.)**

0.1 **At stop light, cross Route 1 to Washington Road.**
Several sprawling horse farms are along this road.

2.2 **Turn right on Central Road (unmarked). You're at Rye Center by a church and town hall.**
This is the historic district of Rye. The Congregational Church in front of you at this turn is over 200 years old. The newly renovated library at this intersection appears in stark contrast to the old town hall and other historic Federal style residences that flank the town common.

4.0 **Go right on Love Lane.**

4.8 **At T-intersection, go right on South Road (unmarked).**

4.9 **Left on Woodland Road.**

6.4 **At stop sign, stay straight on Woodland.**
Little River Cemetery, a lovely old cemetery with beautiful stonework walls, is at this intersection.

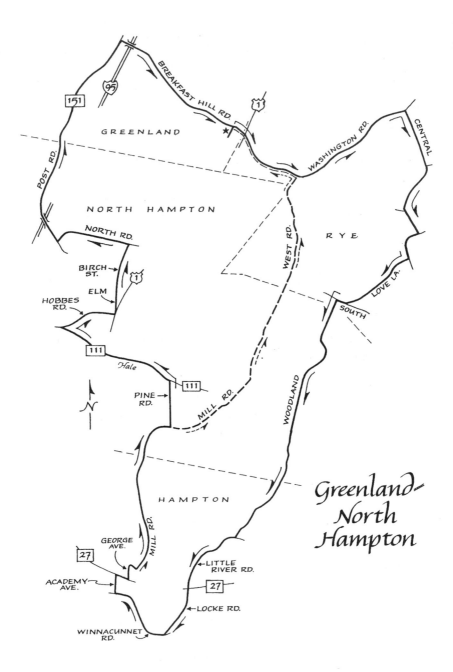

Greenland-
North
Hampton

Shortly after this intersection is a development known as Runnymede, also called Millionaire's Row.

8.2   **At Y-intersection, blend left on Little River Road.**

8.6   **At flashing light, cross High Street to Locke Road.**

9.2   **At stop sign, go right on Winnacunnet Road (unmarked).**

9.9   **Go right on Academy Avenue, just past the court house.**

10.1   **At stop sign/T-intersection, go right on High Street/Route 27 (unmarked).**

10.2   **Go left on George Avenue.**

10.5   **At T intersection, go left on Mill Road (unmarked).**

10.8   **At 4-way stop sign, continue straight on Mill Road.**

12.2   **Go left on Pine Road. (Unless you want a shorter ride.)**

Note: If you want to do a shorter ride, see "Shorter Ride Directions" following.

12.6   **At stop sign/T-intersection, go left on Atlantic Avenue (unmarked).**

13.4   **At stop light, cross Route 1 to Atlantic Avenue/Route 111.**

14.0   **At stop sign/Y-intersection, go right on Hobbs Road (a yellow house is in front of you).**

14.5   **At stop sign/Y intersection, take a sharp left on Elm Street by the large Victorian farm.**

14.7   **Go straight/left on Birch Street (unmarked).**

15.3   **At stop sign/T-intersection, go left on North Road (unmarked).**

You'll pass the Sagamore Golf Course on your right.

16.1   **At stop sign/T-intersection, go right on Post Road/Route 151 (unmarked).**

There's a nice uphill on this road after Sanderson Pond.

In early July, the annual Ultralight Fly-in lasts a week and attracts hundreds of the small open-cockpit planes to the Sanderson Pond Airfield.

18.5   **Go right on Breakfast Hill Road.**

20.0   **Go right into Bethany Church parking lot.**

Shorter Ride Directions
If you'd like to shorten the ride to 16.5 miles:

12.2   **Instead of turning left on Pine Road at 12.2 miles, continue straight on Mill Road (Becomes West Road in Rye).**

At 14.5 miles at the corner of South Road, a 1789 whitewashed, Federal-style colonial graces the corner lot on the left.

A large horse farm spreads out on the right shortly after this. The white paddock fences stretch all around the property.

15.5   **At stop sign/T-intersection, go left on Washington Road (unmarked—Christine's Crossing is at this corner).**

16.3   **At light, cross Route 1 to Breakfast Hill Road.**

16.5   **Left into parking lot at Bethany Church.**

18 | *Four Forts*

Rye–Portsmouth

18.4 miles.
Mostly flat ride.

his ride encompasses four forts along the way. Fort Dearborn. Fort Stark. Great Island Common. Fort Constitution. All have played various roles in the history of the Seacoast and the country at large.

Fort Dearborn is located at Odiorne Point State Park in Rye on the ocean. The park includes the remains of several pieces of American history, from the fishing encampments of the Penacook and Abenaki tribes to the earliest explorations by Giovanni da Verrazano in 1524 to the camouflaged fortifications built here during WWII. They are strange structures—do detour and ride your bikes around them on the paths.

Fort Stark is located on Great Island, more commonly called New Castle, just east of Portsmouth. Originally constructed in 1746, it was rebuilt and updated continually throughout the nation's history. Fort Stark was actively fortified in every war from the American Revolution to WWII, when it was a submarine spotting site. Fort Stark is open on the weekends in the spring and fall, and daily from Memorial Day to Labor Day.

Great Island Common is another fort, but lesser known. Great Island Common (marked Fort Langdon on many maps) used to be a military reservation. A local shared how he remembered as a kid that inmates from the Navy Prison used to be ferried back and forth in WWII landing craft for exercise at Great Island Common. The pier where the landing craft docked still stands there today.

The fourth fort, Fort Constitution, is also located in New Castle. Fort Constitution, a British bastion, was raided by rebel patriots in 1774 and the stolen munitions used against the British at the Battle of Bunker Hill four months later. If you visit Fort Constitution, take the paved walking trail from the fort through the 18th-century town for a close-up look at the former colonial residences that are now private homes. The attraction charges no admission fee.

While pedaling through Portsmouth a few miles into the ride, you pass Strawbery Banke, a 10-acre outdoor museum with period gardens, monthly activities, and more than 40 buildings that date from the years 1695 to 1820. It was named Strawbery Banke by passengers who disembarked from a ship on the east bank of the Piscataqua River in 1630. They found the ground covered with wild strawberries. Hence, the name. The little settlement eventually grew into the seaport of Portsmouth.

Across the street from Strawbery Banke is Prescott Park, where a breathtaking array of thousands of colorful flowers grace the grounds and flank the brick pathways. Also during the summer, the Prescott Park Festival features live performances in its open-air theater for several weeks. No fee is charged, but a donation is suggested.

This historic aspect of the ride is interesting, but the scenery is fierce competition. This is a pretty ride with splendid ocean views and terrific cycling! Enjoy the day.

RIDE INFORMATION

Highlights: Four forts. Historic Portsmouth. Strawbery Banke and Prescott Park. Ice cream stop. Seacoast Science Center. Magnificent Wentworth-by-the-Sea. Pretty cycling along the ocean. Sun bathing at Wallis Sands Beach.

Start: Begin at Wallis Sands Beach Park, located on Route 1A in Rye. This is a bathing beach.

RIDE DIRECTIONS

0.0 **Go right out of the beach parking lot on Route 1A North.**

At 1.5 miles on the right is Odiorne Point State Park.

Fort Dearborn is located here. Also wildlife viewing areas abound. The Seacoast Science Center, an Audubon educational center on the grounds of the park, offers a chance for some wonderful hands on introductions to the sea as well as splendid views of the water.

At 2.3 miles be careful crossing the wooden bridge.

3.4   At stop sign at Foyes Corner, go right, staying on Route 1A.

3.9   Go right on Route 1B North.

At 4.3 miles is the Ice House on your right. A must stop on a hot day!

At about 4.9 miles, walk your bike across the bridge.

Soon you'll see Wentworth-by-the-Sea Hotel on your left. A grand hotel that suffered from disrepair, she was recently renovated to her former grande dame status. Historically the hotel is known for President Theodore Roosevelt's visit in 1905. At this hotel he negotiated and signed the Treaty of Portsmouth, which ended the Russo-Japanese War.

One of many classic photo opportunities New Hampshire offers in abundance.

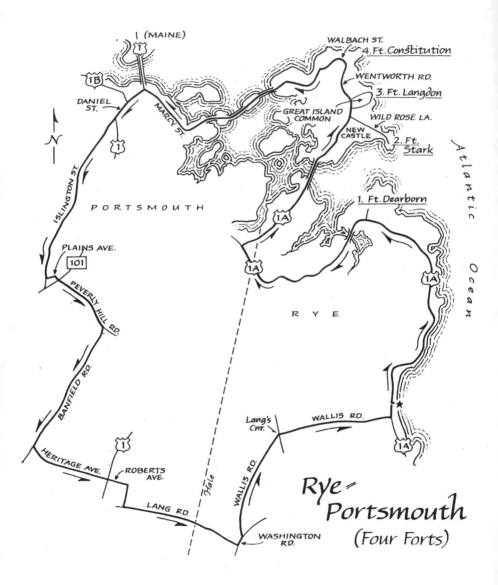

Rye - Portsmouth (Four Forts)

At 5.6 miles, go right on Wild Rose Lane if you want to visit Fort Stark. This is fort 2!

At about 5.8 miles you can see fort 3—Great Island Common—on your right. This used to be a military reservation. (Some maps have it marked as Fort Langdon.) Rest rooms and picnic tables are available here.

6.2 **Go straight on Wentworth Road.**

If you look to your right, you can see fort 4—the coast guard station—Fort Constitution.

6.3 **Road curves to left here onto Walbach Street.**

6.4 **At stop sign, you're back at Route 1B. Go right.**

You're entering New Castle, a small community of about 800 people and some of the most expensive real estate on the Seacoast. Many historic old homes can be seen along 1B. One at the turn here on the right was built in 1755.

At 7.2 miles on your right, you'll see an imposing castle-like structure on the island. It's an abandoned Navy prison that's earmarked for a facelift to eventually become executive office space.

8.2 **At stop sign, go right on Marcy Street.**

8.4 **Go right—still on Marcy Street. Sander's Fish Market is at this corner.**

Soon you're in the historic district of Portsmouth known as Strawbery Banke. Prescott Park is also located here. A visit to the museum shop uncovers an old fashioned candy counter and other delights.

8.8 **At stop sign, go right, and then under bridge.**

8.9 **At stop sign, go straight on Daniel Street.**

You're in the center of downtown Portsmouth and soon you will pass by historic Old North Church and travel on cobblestone streets.

9.3 **At stop light, go straight. This road becomes Islington Street.**

9.9   At stop light at Bartlett Street, stay straight on Islington.
Papa Wheelies Bike Shop is at this corner. Do stop in if you need anything—or to say hi.

11.0   Go left on Plains Avenue by the ball park.

11.1   At stop light, go straight on Peverly Hill Road.

11.8   Go right on Banfield Road.

13.1   Go left on Heritage Avenue.

13.9   At light at Route 1, go straight on Roberts Avenue.
Visit Papa Gino's here if you're starving.

14.2   Take the last right (beyond the boulder) in this apartment complex. You're still on Roberts Avenue.

14.4   At stop sign/T-intersection, go left on Lang Road (unmarked).

15.5   Go left at stop sign on Washington Road.

15.7   The road forks after the school—stay left on Wallis Road.

16.7   At stop sign at Lang's Corner, go straight on Wallis Road.

17.9   Go left at stop sign on Route 1A North.
You can see the ocean ahead of you!

18.4   Back at Wallis Sands Park.

19 *Historic Exeter*

Exeter–Kensington

*15.4 miles. Numerous rolling hills,
but well worth the effort.*

E xeter, NH, once the state capital, offers the visitor a wealth of history that represents the very beginnings of America. The American Independence Museum is sited on two beautiful acres of land in downtown Exeter. Housed in the National Historic Register's Ladd-Gilman House, the museum focuses on the Colonial period and the time of the American Revolution. The museum's historic collection includes two draft copies of the U.S. Constitution with editorial notes.

The 1775 Folsom Tavern, saved from demolition and moved to its present location in 1929, is managed by the museum. A tour of this structure is informative and educational.

The museum is open mid-May to early November, Wednesday through Saturday from 10 A.M. to 4 P.M. There is a fee for the museum tour. For additional information, call (603) 772-2622.

Phillips Exeter Academy, a distinguished prep school, chartered in 1781 (the state's first chartered high school), boasts a rich heritage of academic excellence, and a sprawling campus that features stately brick Georgian and Colonial buildings as well as more contemporary structures like the new $38M Phelps Science Center.

With just over 1,000 students, the school occupies 118 buildings on 1,000 acres of land. Founded by Dr. John Phillips, the school embraces his intent to encourage goodness with knowledge, and develop the consciences and intelligence of the students so that they may serve usefully in our society.

Among the many fine colonial-period and 19th century houses in Exeter, of special note is the Gilman Garrison House, built about 1690. The massive, square-sawn log walls of the house, now clapboarded over, may have been a response to the threats of Indian attack, which was much feared in the Great Bay region before 1713.

The bicycling route, which bears no historic significance, is also noteworthy. This ride is a classic in its own right. Lazy country roads with little traffic calm and soothe the soul. Farm livestock grazing in fields remind you of less-hurried times of yesteryear. And the historic structures and artifacts recall the tenacity and courage of our founding fathers and mothers.

RIDE INFORMATION

Highlights: The American Independence Museum, Phillips Exeter Academy, historic homes, wonderful specialty shops downtown, restaurants worth a stop, and terrific cycling past rolling farmlands, grazing cows, and scenery to die for.

Start: Begin in Exeter at the municipal parking lot downtown across from the Ioka Theater on Water Street.

RIDE DIRECTIONS

0.0   **Take a right on Water Street out of the municipal parking lot.**

You're in the historic district of Exeter at the start of this ride. Wonderful old colonial structures are nearby. From this viewpoint you can also see the bandstand (gazebo) that proudly defies traffic in the middle of Water Street.

0.1   **At stop light, go straight on Route 27/High Street.**

Exeter Cycles is located at this intersection. Do stop in if you need any equipment, energy bars, or just to say hello to John, the owner—one of the friendliest, as well as extremely knowledgeable, bicycling experts around.

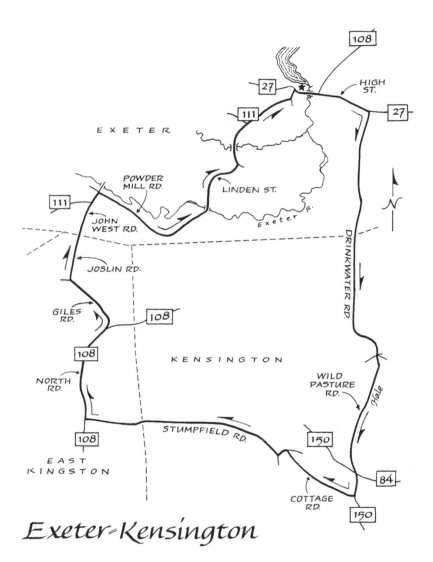

108

27

HIGH
ST.

111

27

EXETER

POWDER
MILL RD.

LINDEN ST.

111

JOHN
WEST RD.

Exeter R.

JOSLIN RD.

N

GILES
RD.

108

DRINKWATER RD.

108

KENSINGTON

WILD
PASTURE
RD.

NORTH
RD.

Hale

108

STUMPFIELD RD.

150

EAST
KINGSTON

84

COTTAGE
RD.

150

Exeter-Kensington

0.8   **Turn right on Drinkwater Road.**

This pretty road, canopied with towering trees which throw lacy patterns across the road, takes you into Kensington. Rock walls, grazing horses, and Kodak-moment working farms offer serene views along the way.

3.1   **Drinkwater bears to left. Don't take North Road. (Landmark: A 1780 colonial home is situated at this corner.)**

3.8   **At this intersection, continue straight—now on Wild Pasture Road.**

5.3   **At stop sign, go left on Route 150 South.**

5.6   **Turn right on Cottage Road.**

Another pretty road with relaxing views.

6.7   **At yield Y-intersection, go right on Stumpfield Road.**

This road leads into East Kensington. A long up-hill along this road is softened a bit by a nice, long downhill!

9.0   **At stop sign-T-intersection, go right on Route 108/North Road.**

10.3   **Left on Giles Road.**

At the 10.7 mile point, sheep, chickens, horses, and other farm animals populate this working farm. Old farm equipment dotting the fields are great subjects for photos.

11.0   **Right on Joslin Road (becomes John West Road in Exeter).**

A bit of a hill on this road.

11.9   **At the stop sign, go straight on Route 111 (unmarked) for a short way.**

12.0   **Right on Powder Mill Road (becomes Linden Street).**

14.8   **At stop sign, go right/straight on Route 111 (Front Street) in downtown Exeter. Stay left toward the gazebo.**

After the stop sign, you're on the campus of Phillips Exeter Academy.

15.4   **By the gazebo, go right on Route 108 North/Water Street a short way up on the right is the Water Street municipal parking lot.**

Wheel Power Bike Shop is on Water Street—last chance to pick up a new mirror or a spare tube.

Lots of funky, neat restaurants are scattered along here—11 Water Street Restaurant, the Loaf & Ladle, The Green Bean, Szechuan Taste, for example. And candy stores, fine craft shops, Water Street Book Store, and more.

Also on this street is the old Ioaka Theater, an independent cinema that even sports an old-fashioned soda fountain! The name came from "I Owe K.A."— the person who originally extended a loan to the owner many years ago to build the theater.

20 | *Kingston State Beach*

Kingston–Sandown

22.4 miles.
Rolling, with lots of moderate uphills.

Historic rural Kingston in southern Rockingham County is an old farming community. One of the oldest New Hampshire towns (said to be fifth), Kingston's charter dates to 1694.

In the past it was a lumber town, later to become a renowned international center for its poultry business. The New Hampshire Red chicken, in demand from 1930 to 1960, was shipped to every part of the U.S., South America, and Europe.

Kingston's most famous historic figure was Declaration of Independence signer, Josiah Bartlett. Also New Hampshire's first governor, Bartlett, came to Kingston at age 21 as a physician. His house on Main Street is a National Historic Landmark and is listed on the National Register of Historic Places.

If you have time, you may want to have lunch at the historic Kingston 1686 House Restaurant. Kingston House's reputation for fine cuisine is rivaled only by its cozy atmosphere, which is enhanced by an original beehive oven, wide pine floor boards, Indian shutters, nine-over-six window panes and a pulpit staircase.

Skirting into nearby Danville and Sandown, this ride is an absolute joy in the fall. It is exquisitely breathtaking with the turning leaves, (often dancing across your path), virtually no traffic, and the classic beauty of New England backroads.

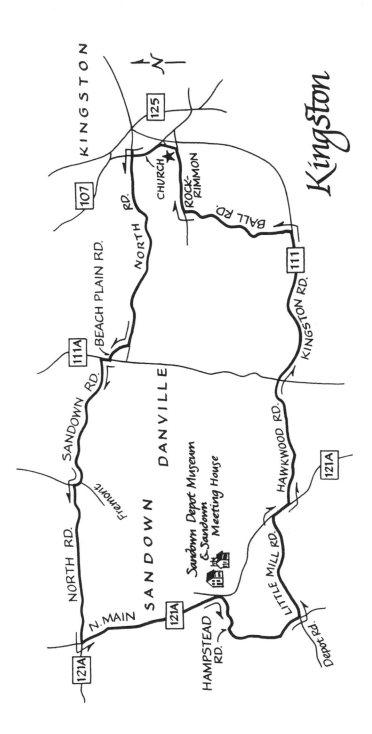

Kingston

This is a super family ride—for older children. It is hilly, so make sure they're ready for it. Let them walk if they need to. You may want to plan a stop afterward at Kingston State Beach for swimming and picnicking.

RIDE INFORMATION

Highlights: One of the oldest towns in the state (Kingston), Josiah Bartlett House, Kingston State Beach.

Start: Kingston Village common. At the village common, park across the street from the fire station or on one of the side roads that intersect the common.

RIDE DIRECTIONS

0.0   **Start the ride from the fire station on Rockrimmon Road. From fire station, go left toward the gazebo.**

At 0.1 mile on left is the Josiah Bartlett House. This home has been continuously lived in by Bartlett's direct descendents, and until 1940 was an active, working farm. On the grounds is a linden tree planted by Dr. Bartlett. It is one of two such trees in Kingston. The other tree is outside Kingston's oldest house, which is part of the Kingston 1686 House Restaurant.

0.2   **Bear left with curve onto Church Street.**

A pizza place and ice cream store are here.

0.7   **Left on North Road.**

3.7   **Bear right on Beach Plain Road.**

4.2   **At stop sign T-intersection go right on Main Street/Route 111A (unmarked) for 0.1 mile.**

4.3   **Left on Sandown Road. (Becomes North Danville Road.)**

6.4   **Turn right on Freemont Road for 0.1 mile.**

6.5   **Left on North Road.**

If you happen to be in this area in early spring, you may be fortunate to cycle past a couple of bogs and catch the "peep, peep, peep" of the spring peeper frogs.

8.9   **At stop sign, left on North Main Street (Route 121A).**
This road has a moderate volume of fast traffic and no breakdown lane. At about the 11.0-mile mark on left is the turn for the Sandown Depot Museum and the historic Sandown Meeting House. Both are on the National Register of Historic Places.

11.1   **Right on Hampstead Road.**

11.8   **Y-intersection, bear left, still on Hampstead Road.**

13.1   **Left on Little Mill.**

14.8   **At stop sign, go right on South Main Street (Route 121A) for 0.3 miles.**
Road has moderate traffic, no breakdown.

15.1   **Left on Hawkewood Road.**

17.1   **At stop sign at intersection, cross Route 111A diagonally to the right. Left on Kingston Road.**
Located at this intersection is Danville Village Market, where you can buy subs and sandwiches.

19.7   **Left on Ball Road.**

21.4   **At stop sign/T intersection, go right on Rockrimmon Road (unmarked).**

22.4   **You're back at the fire station.**
To get to Kingston State Park from here, travel half a mile south (in the opposite direction of the gazebo).

21 *Apple Orchard Ride*

Hampton–Kensington

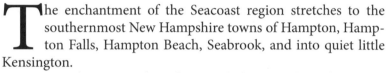

20.7 miles.
Mostly flat with a few short hills.

The enchantment of the Seacoast region stretches to the southernmost New Hampshire towns of Hampton, Hampton Falls, Hampton Beach, Seabrook, and into quiet little Kensington.

Hampton has a reputation for crowded streets along the boardwalk, slow-moving "loop" traffic, and a less-than-exciting travel destination—except for the twenty-somethings. Well, think again. We won't be near the beach for this ride.

But we will be cruising along pretty tree-lined roads, past rock walls, apple orchards, and white paddock fences. We skirt crystal clear ponds, view Great Blue Herons fishing for lunch, and pedal past picturesque horse farms. Not what you thought for Hampton? That's OK. Life is sometimes learning to stretch beyond expectations. And this ride should fulfill even the highest expectations—for a scenic foray into parts of the Seacoast which are best known by area cyclists who prefer to keep the terrific, lesser-traveled backroads a bit to themselves. I don't blame them. But this one we'll share.

Although the ride begins in a busier part of Hampton, you soon meander on to quieter backroads in Hampton Falls, Kensington, and back again. Hampton Falls is a picture-postcard example of New England—especially along the roads we travel on this bike ride. The town was originally a part of Hampton, but was incorpo-

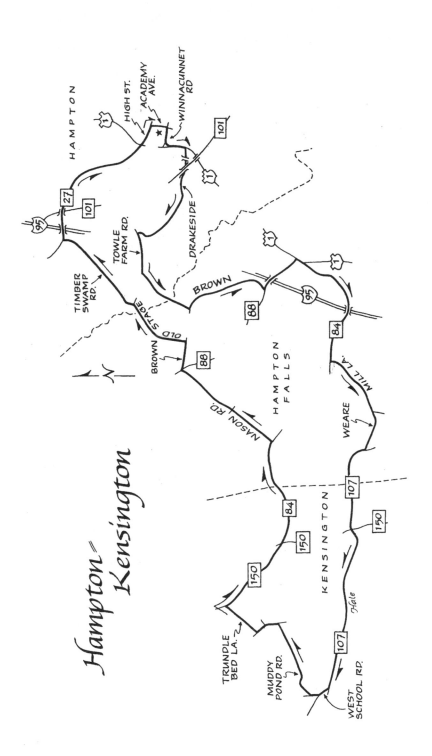

Hampton–
Kensington

rated as a separate community in 1726. Today, many old buildings and stately farms stand as a testament to its colorful past.

Winding country roads lead past sprawling farms and well-kept farmhouses—the kind that reminds you of your grandparents and slower, simpler times. Residents and visitors alike await the changing of the seasons to visit the abundant apple and berry orchards throughout the Hampton Falls and Kensington countryside.

Whoever heard of Kensington? It's not well known. But the quiet community of Kensington knows exactly what its doing. It knows a good thing when it sees it! But even so, Kensington is being discovered. An increase in new housing developments dot the landscape, and so this beautiful rural area falls prey to population expansion and peoples' desire to be near the Seacoast.

This ride is really a pretty trip and skirts past numerous apple orchards, horse paddocks, vine-covered rock walls, and ponds teeming with wildlife. Best of all, the route offers terrific cycling.

RIDE INFORMATION

Highlights: Rock walls, apple orchards, paddock fences, ponds, Great Blue Herons, horse farms.

Start: Begin at the corner of Winnacunnet Road and Academy Avenue (by Hampton's Lane Library). Winnacunnet Road is just off Route 1 by the Galley Hatch Restaurant.

RIDE DIRECTIONS

0.0   **Right out of District Court parking on Winnacunnet Road.**

0.2   **Go left at fork to stop sign, then left on Route 1 South.**
The Galley Hatch Restaurant on Route 1 is an icon on the Seacoast. With a varied, interesting menu, and a bakery chockful of pastries and cakes to die for, it is worth a look-see and a stop for lunch.

0.5   **Go right on Drakeside.**

1.8   **At stop sign/T-intersection, go left on Towle Farm Road (unmarked).**

3.0   At stop sign/T-intersection, go left on Brown Road (unmarked, corn field ahead of you, big farm house on left).

4.1   At stop sign/T-intersection, go left on Route 88 (unmarked).

4.6   At stop light near the gazebo, go right on Route 1 South (Hampton Falls Center), then a quick right on Route 84 (Kensington Road).

Stately properties line this country road.

6.3   Go left on Mill Lane.

A pond is on your right.

7.1   At Y-intersection bear right on Weare (unmarked).

7.7   At stop sign/T-intersection, go right on Route 107 (unmarked).

8.6   At stop sign/blinking light, continue straight on Route 107 North.

At the 10.1 mile mark, note the white Federal-style colonial home set back from the road that was built in 1725. Federal is a classic architectural style that stands in good stead—even, indeed, in our new millennium.

10.7   Go right on West School Road. (Becomes Muddy Pond Road.)

A hill soon greets you on this pretty, tree-lined road. Hang in there—what goes up, must come down!

10.8   Bear right with curve.

11.8   At fork, stay left on Stumpfield Road.

12.1   Go right on Trundle Bed Lane.

12.5   At stop sign/T-intersection, go right on Route 150 (unmarked).

This is a pretty road—makes the ride all the more enjoyable.

13.5   Go left on Route 84.

Tall, stately pines flank this shady lane.

14.7   Go left on Nason (unmarked, there's a farm on your right here with a wooden fence).

15.3   At 4-way stop sign, go straight on Nason (unmarked).

16.1   At stop sign-T-intersection, go right on Route 88, then an immediate left on Brown (unmarked).

16.4   Left on Old Stage Road.

Apple orchards along this road show off their pink splendor in the spring and offer succulent red fruit in the fall.

The bridge at 17.2 miles on this road is closed to car traffic, but is passable by bike. On the other side, you'll come out by a working (and smelly!) farm.

17.3   At Y intersection, turn left on Timber Swamp Road (unmarked).

18.5   Right on Route 27.

20.3   At light at intersection of Route 1/Route 27 (same as High Street), continue straight on High Street.

20.5   Right on Academy Avenue.

20.7   Left to District Court.

22 *Hampton's North Beach*

Hampton's North Beach–Exeter

20.2 miles.
Mostly flat, a few short hills.

Although this ride bears all the earmarks of a classic New England bike ride—stone walls, apple orchards in bloom, pastoral scenery, and ocean views—it is not a good choice for the timid rider. Some of the roads on this tour have fast traffic, depending on when you ride. So keep that in mind and if you're a newbie rider, do this ride during a weekday morning or early in the spring.

For the more seasoned rider or more adventurous, confident rider, this is a tour worth repeating. Beginning at Hampton's North Beach, the ride rolls through Hampton Falls, Exeter, Stratham, and back to the ocean at North Beach.

The apple orchards along the way present a colorful display of pink blossoms in the spring, or in the fall, the sweet smell of ripe apples tempt you to stop by one of the "U-Pik" farms, buy some of the yummy fruit, and go home and make apple crisp later—a just reward for the riding workout!

Nothing beats the ocean views as you near the shore along Atlantic Avenue. The elevated panoramic shots of the awesome Atlantic Ocean are a trip highlight.

One last thought—don't miss The Beach Plum. It's an age-old landmark in North Hampton, and by all means a "must-do" for ice cream. You can have lunch there before you leave on your ride, and when you're done, treat yourself to their terrific ice cream.

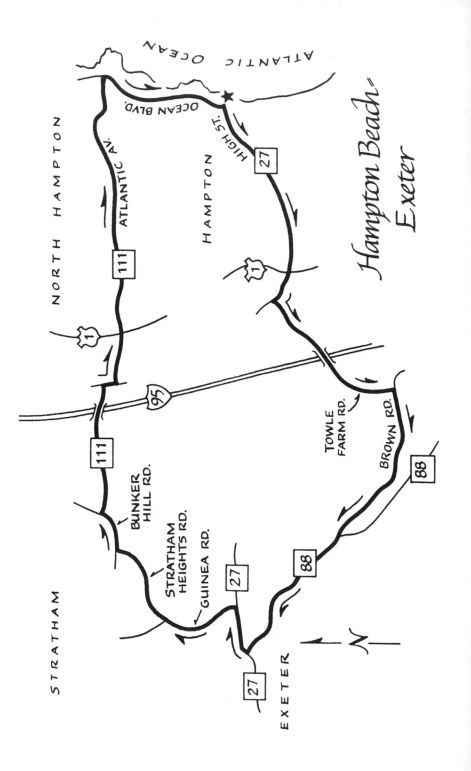

Hampton Beach-
Exeter

RIDE INFORMATION

Highlights: Apple orchards, pastoral farm scenes, ocean views, old graveyards, stone walls, easy riding.

Start: North Beach in Hampton. At Route 1 (Ocean Blvd.) and Route 27 (High Street).

RIDE DIRECTIONS

0.0 **Head west on Route 27 (High Street).**
Cinnamon Rainbows Surf Company is at this intersection. Great for renting a surfboard and trying a new sport!

2.3 **Stop light at Route 1. Stay straight on Route 27W. Caution. Very busy intersection.**

2.8 **Left on Towle Farm Road.**
At 2.9 miles there's a convenience store. Across from it is a pond and relaxation area.

4.9 **At stop sign/T-intersection, right on Brown Road (unmarked).**
Apple trees line both sides of the road.

5.6 **At stop sign, right on Route 88 (unmarked).**
At 7.2 miles is the Tilton House, a Federal-style colonial home with a center chimney built in 1740.

9.1 **Right on Route 27. (Busy road, but has a wide breakdown lane.)**

9.8 **Left on Guinea Road.**

10.6 **At stop sign/V-intersection, go right on Stratham Heights Road (unmarked). A stone wall at this turn.**

11.9 **Right on Bunker Hill Road.**

14.3 **At T-intersection yield sign, go right on Post Road. (Same as Route 151, unmarked).**

14.4 **Left on Route 111E (Atlantic Avenue) by the church. Stay on Route 111E all the way to the ocean.**
At Route 111 and Route 1 is Ronaldo's Restaurant in the plaza. Excellent Italian food.
At 15.5 miles Joe's Meat Market is worth a stop. Fresh produce and delightful homemade pies and pastries.

Along Atlantic Avenue you'll see very exclusive Seacoast estates, and as you near Atlantic Avenue, breathtaking ocean views!

18.5   Right on Route 1-A/Ocean Boulevard.

An ice cream stop is in order at the 19-mile point.

And don't miss the multi-million dollar ocean-front homes along this road.

20.2   Back where you began.

If you're dying for ice cream or a lobster roll, continue up the road another mile or so (still on Route 1A/Ocean Blvd.) to The Beach Plum on your left. It's certainly worth the ride.

This is one of many stone walls you will pedal past in the pricey neighborhoods you ride through on this bike ride.

Linda Chestney

23 *Fall Foliage Ride*

Hampton Falls–Kensington

9.7 miles.
Rolling with a few moderate hills.

Although lesser-known areas of New Hampshire, Hampton Falls and Kensington are nevertheless blessed with some terrific roads for bike riding.

The canopy of tall trees, coupled with the lichen-covered stone walls along these country back roads quickly ease stress and replace it with an inner calm. Soon the apple orchards and bright, white horse paddocks that you're zipping past, remind you of what a gift it is to live in New Hampshire—or if you're visiting, why you came here in the first place. It is the perfect fall foliage tour (or really, any season in New Hampshire offers its own charm).

Hampton Falls is known for its antique shops. You can find anything from conventional antique items here to unusual architectural appointments—such as balusters, carved doors, and stained glass windows.

Kensington is a bedroom community that offers many less-traveled roads for cycling. Nearby is Seabrook, where you can visit the Science and Nature Center on Route 1 at Seabrook Station. Here, the kiddies can observe aquariums with live sea life or explore a salt marsh on a self-guided tour.

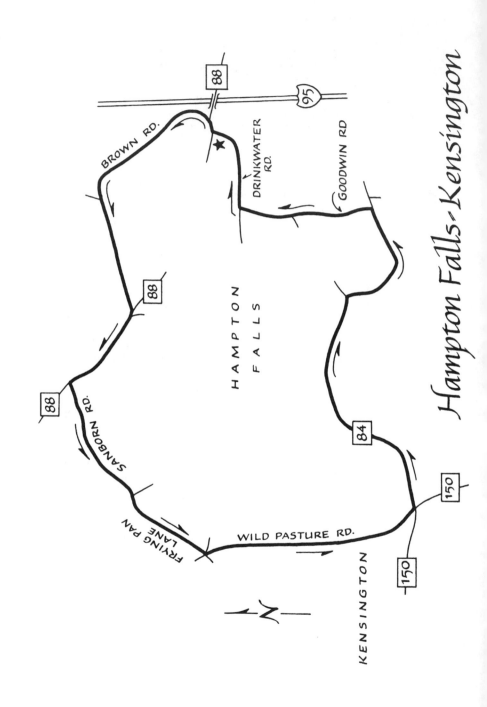

Hampton Falls-Kensington

RIDE INFORMATION

Highlights: Short ride. Good for early in the season. Apple orchards and raspberry farms for picking. Historic buildings. Scenic—duck ponds, cows grazing, picturesque farm properties. Antique shops and the ocean nearby.

Start: Hampton Falls Town Hall. From Route 1, take Route 88W for 0.6 miles. Town hall on left.

RIDE DIRECTIONS

0.0 **Leave town hall parking lot, turn right on Route 88E.**

Hampton Falls Town Hall, a two-story structure with simple Palladian windows, was built in 1877. Restorations 20 years ago uncovered original two-armed, gas lights with etched glass globes. They were then wired for electricity and currently are in full use in the Town Hall meeting room. Also in this room is an antique Seth Thomas clock. Original deacons benches also add charm to the colonial starkness of this building.

Across the street is the Hampton Falls Free Library, constructed in 1901. Inside a chandelier, which used to grace the foyer of the town hall, adds to the beauty of the exterior Corinthian columns and exquisite stained glass elliptical fanlight with sidelights.

0.1 **Left on Brown Road.**

Photo opp: Don't miss the duck ponds with accommodating subjects for photographs. Also wonderful, comfortable old farm houses dot this road, where Holstein cows teach subtle lessons about life's busyness. And, depending on the time of year, you may encounter the apple trees in glorious bloom, or smell the sweet, ripe fruit, ready for picking.

1.9 **At stop sign, right on Route 88W (unmarked).**

At 2.5 miles on the right is Applecrest Farm. Pick some apples and make a pie for your grandmother!

2.6   **Left on Sanborn Road.**
You'll love this road. No traffic. The scent and sight of the towering evergreen trees and hardwood trees throwing lacy patterns in your path. Stone walls. And a chance to see some pricey, upscale homes.

3.5   **At T, right on Frying Pan Lane.**

4.0   **CAUTION—road becomes gravel for 0.1 mile.**

4.1   **Cross the tarred road and go left on Wild Pasture Road.**

5.6   **At stop sign, left on Route 84E. (This is a weird little jog.)**

8.3   **Left on Goodwin Road.**

9.1   **At stop sign/T-intersection, right on Drinkwater Road (unmarked).**

9.7   **Left into town hall parking lot.**

24 *Four Hamptons*

Hampton–North Hampton–
Hampton Falls–South Hampton

22.1 miles. Mostly flat.
Easy riding. Some roads lack a breakdown.

T he Hamptons. We have numerous "Hamptons" in New
Hampshire. Five actually. Hampton, North Hampton,
South Hampton, Hampton Falls, and New Hampton. This
ride rolls through four of the "Hampton" towns. We don't hit New
Hampton, as it's not even on the Seacoast. It is actually up north in
the Lakes region, near Meredith. But the rest of the Hamptons are
terrific for cycling.

You start near busy Route 1 in Hampton, but quickly skirt into
North Hampton, Hampton Falls, and South Hampton.

Easy country lanes lead us past dairy farms, grazing cows, spar-
kling clear ponds, and remote birch stands tucked back into the
rolling landscape. All make for scenic, leisurely cycling in one of
the prettiest corners of New Hampshire.

RIDE INFORMATION

Highlights: Lots of farms. Cows grazing. Horse farms. Duck
ponds. Rock walls. Relatively easy riding. Shady
lanes. Ice cream stops! Little traffic.

Start: Begin at the corner of Winnacunnet Road and
Academy Avenue (by Hampton's Lane Library) in
Hampton. Winnacunnet Road is just off Route 1
by the Galley Hatch Restaurant.

RIDE DIRECTIONS

0.0   **Go left on Winnacunnet Road.**

0.1   **Go left to Mill Road stop sign.**

1.9   **Go left on Cedar Road.**
          You've crossed over into North Hampton now.

2.5   **At stop sign, go right on Route 1, then an immediate left by the Golden Garden Restaurant on South Road.**

2.7   **At stop sign/T-intersection, go left on Route 151/Post Road (unmarked), and then an immediate right—staying on South Road.**

4.3   **At stop sign, go left on Route 111 (unmarked).**
This is a busy road, but has a breakdown lane.

6.0   **At stop sign, go right—on Route 27/Route 111.**

6.2   **Go left on Ashbrook. (You're now in Exeter.)**
At this corner is Lee Mac's Market. Ice cream stop!

6.8   **At stop sign, go left on Route 88 (unmarked). In front of you is a sign: Exeter Falls Development.**

David Gish

This is a busy road with no breakdown lane. You cycle past scenic farms, ponds with jumping frogs, and lichen-covered stone walls. You've now passed into Hampton Falls.

8.6   Go right on Sanborn.

A gorgeous country road with the sun breaking through the leafy trees and throwing lacy patterns on the road, this shady lane is a cyclist's delight.

9.5   Go right on Frying Pan Lane. This road becomes gravel at the end for 0.1 of a mile.

Some pricey houses line this road.

10.1   Cross the road to the stop sign, and go left on Wild Pasture Road.

A pretty, tree-lined road.

11.6   At stop sign, go straight on Route 150. (This is actually a slight left—about 11 o'clock.)

This road has no breakdown.

At 12.6 miles is the Twin Lantern Dairy Bar. Ice cream!

13.3   Go left on Locust Street.

You're now in South Hampton, traveling along another pretty, tree-lined road.

14.0   At 3-way stop sign/T-intersection, go left on Blacksnake (unmarked).

14.2   Go left on True Road.

14.8   At T-intersection, go right on New Zealand (unmarked, there is a short rock wall in front of you here).

15.2   At stop sign, go right on Route 107 (unmarked—near Seabrook Dog Track).

This is a busy road.

15.3   Go left on Weare Road.

15.6   At stop sign/T-intersection, go right on Mill Lane.

Mill Lane is a pretty, shaded road and soon—a nice downhill!

16.5   At stop sign/T-intersection, go left on Route 84 (un-

marked).

16.6 **Go right on Goodwin Road (becomes Crank Road).**

17.4 **At stop sign/T-intersection, go right on Drinkwater Road (unmarked—a rock wall here on both sides of the road).**

18.0 **At stop sign, go right on Route 88 (unmarked), and immediate left on Brown Road at 18.1 miles.**

You're now in Hampton Falls.

At the 18.4 mile point, a duck pond with lots of ducks is on the right. On the left is a horse farm.

19.1 **Go right on Towle Farm Road (unmarked—big farm house at this corner. Corn field in front of you).**

You're back in Hampton. Ya-hoo—all four Hamptons in an hour or less!

At 21.0 miles the Towle Farm Market is on right. Great stopping place for refreshments. Take your goodies across the road to the duck pond, grab a park bench, and watch the waterfowl cavort.

21.2 **At stop sign/T-intersection, go right on Route 27/High Street (unmarked).**

21.7 **At stop light on Route 1, go straight on High Street.**

Zesto's Pizza is at this corner. Yum! Me & Ollie's just ahead.

21.9 **Go right on Academy Avenue.**

22.1 **At stop sign, go left on Winnicunnet Road. You're back at the library on left.**

25 Merrimac River Ride

Hampton, NH–West Newbury, MA

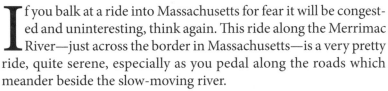

38.4 miles.

I f you balk at a ride into Massachusetts for fear it will be congested and uninteresting, think again. This ride along the Merrimac River—just across the border in Massachusetts—is a very pretty ride, quite serene, especially as you pedal along the roads which meander beside the slow-moving river.

If you're lucky, you might even see deer grazing in an open meadow along the river. The day we rode this ride, we spotted—a ways back from the road—three deer eating while keeping a wary eye on us. It was a real treat.

The Maudslay State Park is also a destination to consider. The Moseley Estate, known as Maudsleigh from the 1860s to the 1970s, is known today as Maudslay State Park. One of the wealthiest families in New England, the Moseleys hired Charles Sprague Sargeant and Martha Brooks Hutcheson (one of the first female landscape architects) to shape the grounds of their estate. These spectacular grounds and gardens are now open to the public. Hikers will enjoy this new park along the heights above the Merrimac River in Newburyport. Picnic tables are also available.

Once a shipbuilding center, Newburyport is the birthplace of the U.S. Coast Guard. Built in the 1650s, the Coffin House (at 14 High Street) reflects the many generations of residency by the Coffin family. Guided tours are given on weekends in the summer. Phone (978) 462-2634.

If you'd like to take a side tour, check out the Custom House Maritime Museum on Water Street. A Classic Revival-style custom house built in 1835, it houses exhibits that pertain to more than 300 years of maritime history, the China trade, and shipbuilding on the Merrimac River. A 15-minute AV program gives visitors an overview of the history of Newburyport. Tues.–Sun., 10–4. Admission fee of $7. Call (978) 462-8681 if you have questions.

RIDE INFORMATION

Highlights: Pretty ride wends along the river banks of Merrimac River in Massachusetts. Apple orchards. Maudslay State Park. Old cemeteries and weathered stone walls. Possible deer sighting. Active sheep farm.

Start: Begin at Park & Ride in Hampton located at Routes 27 and I-95.

RIDE DIRECTIONS

0.0 **Go left out of parking lot on Timber Swamp Road.**
Timber Swamp Road is a pretty, tree-lined road. Cornstalks sway in the summer breeze as you pedal past a working farm with silo. It *is* a working farm—you'll detect that by the smell.

1.1 **At fork, go left—still on Timber Swamp Road.**

1.4 **At stop sign, go right on Towle Farm Road.**

1.9 **At stop sign/T-intersection, go left on Brown Road (unmarked).**

2.9 **At stop sign/T-intersection, go left on Route 88 East.**

3.4 **Go right at traffic light on Route 1 South.**
You're now in Hampton Falls.

3.5 **Go right/straight on Route 84 West.**
Pretty properties flank this road. A rustic bridge with a flowing creek beneath invite a stop for an energy bar break.

4.6 **At first left beyond I-95, go left on Stard Road (unmarked).**

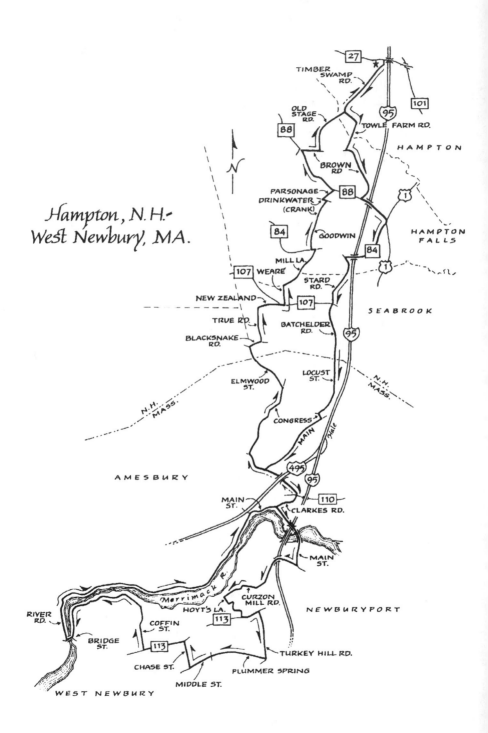

Hampton, N.H.-
West Newbury, MA.

5.6 At stop light, cross Route 107, to continue straight on Batchelder Road (becomes Locust Street).

7.8 At stop sign/T-intersection, go left on Congress Street (unmarked).

7.9 At stop sign, go right on Main/Monroe Streets (unmarked).

8.9 At the first left after the industrial park, go left on Portsmouth Road.

9.4 At stop sign/T-intersection at Elm Street (unmarked), go left.

9.9 At stop light cross Route 110, and stay straight on Clarkes Road.

> Friendly's is at this corner—in case you want to grab a bite to eat or indulge in a chocolate ice cream cone!

> Farther along on this road on the right, is an attractive old burying ground with many lichen-covered grave stones.

10.4 Go left on Main Street (unmarked).

10.6 At stop sign/T-intersection, go right on Old Main Street.

> The river is directly ahead of you at this stop sign.

10.8 At T-intersection, go left on Old Main Street (unmarked).

10.9 Go right on Main Street.

11.0 At stop sign to the right of the traffic light, turn right on Merrill/Spofford Streets (unmarked).

> CAUTION: Two bridges are ahead—immediately after each other. WALK your bikes!

11.7 At stop sign/T-intersection, at the top of the hill just before stop sign, go right. A sign here says State Park.

12.7 Go right.

12.9 Go straight on Curzon Mill Road.

> Maudslay State Park is on this road. Rest rooms are at the rear of the park's parking lot.

> This is a pretty road flanked on both sides by towering pines and weathered stone walls.

13.0   Turn left on Hoyt's Lane.

Hoyt's Lane is a perfect road for cycling—wooded and meandering along pretty scenery.

13.6   At stop sign/T-intersection, turn left on Route 113 East (unmarked).

13.8   Go right on Turkey Hill Road.

14.7   At stop sign/T-intersection, take a sharp right (the 9 o'clock position) on Plummer Spring (unmarked).

You'll see the river on your left. This tree-lined road has a few scattered houses, a birch stand in the distance in an open field, and little traffic, so you can focus on the scenery.

15.8   At stop sign at Garden Street (unmarked), go straight on Middle Street.

Bends and turns in this tree-lined road add to its charm.

16.3   Go right on Chase Street (unmarked).

An old cemetery on the right is constructed of weathered stones to create an attractive, rustic stone wall.

16.8   At stop sign/T-intersection, go left on Route 113 West (unmarked).

Nice down hill!

17.6   Take a right on Coffin Street.

This road is rough, but soon the views will be worth it.

Coffin Street is a pretty, curving road with nice homes. The road becomes River Road when it bends to the left at the river. This road is bumpy in places. The river escorts you along on the right.

At 19.0 miles on your left is an active sheep farm.

At 20.3 miles on the left is an open field. The day we were riding past here at around 4 P.M., three deer were grazing in the meadow. What a treat! Hope you are as lucky!

20.7   At stop sign/T-intersection, go right on Bridge Street (unmarked).

21.0   After crossing the bridge, turn right on River Road.

22.8   Turn right on River Road.

26.4   At stop sign, turn right on Main Street.

27.2   Go left on Clarks Road.

      A short uphill greets you after the turn.

27.6   At street light at Route 110, go straight on Elm Street (unmarked).

28.2   Go right on Amidon Avenue—the second right beyond I-495.

28.4   At stop sign, go straight on Madison Street.

29.0   At four corners, go right on Congress Street (unmarked—landmark: a white picket fence across the street before the turn).

30.0   At the fork, go left on Elmwood Street.

30.3   Go left—still on Elmwood Street.

31.2   At stop sign, go right on Blacksnake Road (unmarked).

31.4   Turn left on True Road.

32.0   At T-intersection, go right on New Zealand Road (unmarked).

32.4   At stop sign, go right on Route 107 South. (Landmark: Seabrook Dog Track here.)

32.5   Go left on Weare Road.

32.8   At stop sign, go right on Mill Lane.

33.6   At stop sign, go left on Route 84 West (unmarked).

33.7   Go right on Goodwin Road (becomes Crank Road).

34.7   At stop sign, go left on Drinkwater Road (unmarked), then at first right, go right on Parsonage Road.

35.1   At stop sign, go left on Route 88 West.

      Apple orchards will appear along this road. You've entered Hampton Falls.

36.0   At stop sign to the right of the traffic island, go right on Brown Road.

36.3   Go left on Old Stage Road.

37.2   At stop sign to the left of the traffic island, go left on Timber Swamp Road.

38.4   On right is Park & Ride.

26 *Hodgie's Ice Cream*

Newton, NH–Amesbury, MA

16.8 miles.
Rolling, lots of annoying, gradual hills.

Tiny Newton, New Hampshire, which borders Massachusetts, is nestled between South Hampton and Kingston, New Hampshire. A quiet community of mostly commuters, Newton is a haven of little-known backroads and pretty scenery.

Leaving the starting point, you skirt past pretty Lake Attitash and then meander along wooded roads, open fields, and through this undiscovered area of the state. Even though busy Massachusetts roadways are nearby, you avoid them on this bike ride and pedal through small neighborhoods and past rolling farmlands instead.

The Newton couple who designed this ride, Doug and Cheryl Thompson, say not to miss the ice cream stop at Hodgies! You will have earned it with all the pedaling you will be doing—not to mention that the lure of cold ice cream on a warm summer day is irresistible!

The bike ride crosses the border into Amesbury and Merrimac, MA, then you're soon back in the woods pedaling by marshy areas where Great Blue Herons fish for their lunch.

RIDE INFORMATION

Highlights: Lake Attitash, a glimpse of a Great Blue Heron or two, pretty scenery, ice cream stop at Hodgie's!

Start: Begin at Rowes Corner Market on Route 108 in Newton. Park your car toward the back of the building.

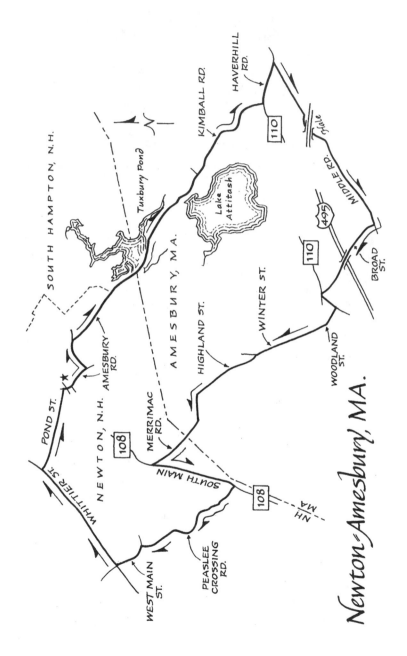

SOUTH HAMPTON, N.H.

Tuxbury Pond

KIMBALL RD.

HAVERHILL RD.

110

Hale

MIDDLE RD.

Lake Attitash

495

110

BROAD ST.

AMESBURY, M.A.

AMESBURY RD.

NEWTON, N.H.

POND ST.

WINTER ST.

HIGHLAND ST.

WOODLAND ST.

MERRIMAC RD.

108

SOUTH MAIN

108

NH
MA

WHITTIER ST.

WEST MAIN ST.

PEASLEE CROSSING RD.

Newton-Amesbury, MA.

RIDE DIRECTIONS

0.0   **Take a right on Route 108S/North Main Street out of the parking lot of Rowes Corner Market. Then take an almost immediate left/straight on Amesbury Road.**

0.3   **Go left—still on Amesbury Road.**

Shortly on the left is Lake Attitash, a pretty lake that looks like little more than a pond from the road. The day we cycled past, a Great Blue Heron was poised at the edge of the water waiting for fish or frogs, its principal food.

3.2   **At stop sign, continue straight now on Kimball Road.**

4.5   **At stop sign, go left on Route 110/Haverhill Road.**

New Hampshire has rich colonial roots. White steepled, clapboarded, churches are typical small town architecture around the state.

David Gish

5.0   **Turn right on Middle Road.**

Hodgie's Ice Cream stand is at this corner! Definitely worth a stop.

Soon you'll encounter an annoying gradual uphill on this road.

7.2   **Go right on Broad Street.**

8.3   **At stop sign/T-intersection, left on Route 110 North.** This gets tricky, so pay attention. Continue on Route 110 through a congested downtown intersection of Merrimac, MA (lots of brick buildings here). Then about a block up (still on Route 110) turn right at 8.6 miles on the unmarked street that has a sign that says, "Merrimac Soccer Field." (Across the street from Locust Street) Shortly after you turn on this street, there's a stop sign. Continue straight.

8.8   **At "one o'clock," go right on Woodland/Winter Street.**

9.5   **At T-intersection, go left. Street sign says Winter Street/ Church Street. After the turn, street becomes Highland Street. When it crosses the state line back into New Hampshire, the road becomes Merrimac Road.**

11.2   **At curve, bear to right—still on Merrimac Street.**

11.6   **At stop sign, go left on South Main Street/Route 108 (unmarked).**

12.6   **Go right on Peaslee Crossing Road.**

14.0   **At curve, stay left on West Main Street.**

14.3   **Right on Whittier Street.**

15.2   **Go straight—still on Whittier. (Don't take the right on Highland.)**

15.7   **At Y, bear right on Pond Street.**

16.8   **Back at Rowes Corner Market.**

27 Massachusetts Farm Country

Seabrook, NH–Amesbury, MA

22.5 miles.
Rolling farmland, numerous hills.

Seabrook, New Hampshire, probably best known for its nuclear plant and strip malls along Route 1, is also a nice starting point for leisurely bike rides along the New Hampshire sea shore or the quiet countryside of Massachusetts.

Although this ride starts in the busy Route 1 area, very shortly you'll be in impressed with the quiet countryside you quickly find yourself in—tree-canopied roads, cows grazing, and well, simply, just pretty scenery!

Seabrook is home to the Science and Nature Center at Seabrook Station. A terrific stop for kids (or adults of the curious nature) to learn about energy, electricity, science, and wildlife. Aquariums and a touch pool are featured. Bus tours visit the power plant site and the training center simulator, an exact replica of Seabrook Station's control room.

The Owascoag Trail is a 0.7-mile self-guided nature walk through salt marshes and woods. A picnic area is also available. All are free.

The best part of this loop ride is the scenery. It's a bit challenging for the beginner cyclist (or early in the cycling season) as there are a number of hills, but the pretty scenery, winding roads, charming ambiance, rolling landscapes, are even worth walking your bike for! Don't miss out on this ride because of the hills! Walk your bikes if you want—hey, you're *still* getting exercise! Ride on!

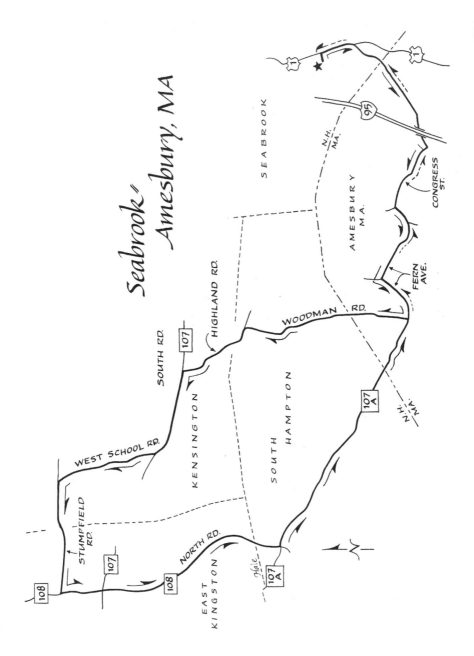

Seabrook–*Amesbury, MA*

RIDE INFORMATION

Highlights: Gorgeous country scenery. Half a dozen historic colonial homes along the bike route. Terrific shopping along Route 1 (and no sales tax in NH!). Science and Nature Center and Owascoag Nature Trail. Picnic area.

Start: Park at Seabrook Community Center in Seabrook at 311 Lafayette Road (Route 1) near Wal-Mart.

RIDE DIRECTIONS

0.0   Go right out of parking lot on Route 1. Busy traffic.

0.5   Go straight—following signs for I-95 (entering Salisbury, MA)—don't go around the traffic circle.

1.3   At stop light, go straight.

1.5   Right on Route 286W.

1.9   Right on Congress Street.

Along this road, cows graze on the hill, while the calves stay nearby, reluctant to stray far from their mothers. White paddock fences complete the picture-perfect scene.

An old barn shows off its partriotic roots.

David Gish

2.9   **At Y, stay left on Congress Street.**

3.1   **Right on Fern Avenue. (The street sign is on the post on left after you turn.)**

> At 3.9 miles, the Cider Hill Farm Country Store sells plants, strawberries, peaches, blueberries, apples, sweet corn, and other goodies. Pick some up for dinner tonight!
>
> This road meanders past a huge farm with lambs and sheep grazing, and later past a pricey neighborhood with large homes. A few hills are encountered—but let the fieldstone walls and leafy trees overhead distract you.

4.0   **At stop sign, go straight, staying on Fern Avenue.**

> You'll encounter a gradual uphill on this road.

4.5   **At T-intersection, go right on Route 107A (unmarked).**

4.9   **Turn right on Woodman Road.**

> This is a rolling, pretty road. Keep an eye out for the marsh at about 6.5 miles on the left. The day we pedaled past a Great Blue Heron was fishing for frogs and small fish. Also a swan inhabits this pond. Gorgeous homes flank this quiet, rural road.

6.8   **At stop sign/T-intersection, go left on Highland Road.**

> At this intersection, don't miss the spreading maple tree across the street on right at the Abraham Brown home. This circa 1720 green Federal-style colonial is one of many historic gems tucked away in the Massachusetts countryside.
>
> This is a hilly road. At 7.4 miles, you'll climb a winding hill for 0.3 of a mile.

7.8   **At stop sign/T-intersection, turn left on South Road (Route 107) unmarked.**

> At 8.1 miles on the right, is a 1725 whitewashed Federal-style home. And soon—a long downhill!

8.6   **Turn right on West School Road.**

8.7 **Stay right at sharp curve.**

A couple of small hills will appear like magic on this road.

9.8 **Road curves, stay left on Stumpfield Road.**

On your right along this road is another historic home, the Chase House, circa 1730. This road also sports some pricey, newer homes.

Shortly, a long uphill challenges you. Think about the top of the hill where a gorgeous, well-kept farm resides. In the spring and summer, the stone wall along the property proudly displays a huge swath of colorful tulips!

Soon a working farm on the left may show off its wares (if the season is right)—rows and rows of rolled hay bales—an important ingredient for livestocks' well-rounded diet.

12.2 **At the stop sign/T-intersection, turn left on North Road/ Route 108.**

12.6 **At the blinking red light, cross Route 107 to South Road.**

More sheep and lambs graze along this country road.

14.7 **At stop sign, go left on 107A/Main Street. The road has no breakdown.**

At 16.9 miles, the farmstand has super tomatoes and sweet corn. We had some for supper!

17.9 **Turn left on Fern Avenue. You'll be backtracking from here to the start.**

At this turn, another gracious Federal-style 1820 colonial home painted yellow and boasting double chimneys resides.

18.3 **At stop sign, cross Market Street (unmarked). Still on Fern Avenue.**

19.2 **At stop sign, go left on Congress Street (unmarked).**

19.5 **At curve, stay right.**

20.4   At stop sign/T-intersection, go left by Bartlett's Farm Stand.

20.9   At stop light, turn left on Route 1/Main Street. Follow Route 1 back into Seabrook. (Go around the circle staying on Route 1N.)

22.5   Seabrook Community Center on your left.

Hampton, NH–Salisbury, MA

20.1 miles.
Mostly flat riding.

The psyche is healed by expansive ocean views and the gentle pounding of the surf. This ride offers a chance to soothe the soul and delight the eye—because it meanders past miles of ocean views!

Starting in Hampton, the ride drops down into Salisbury, Massachusetts, and then flanks the ocean for a long expanse of the ride. Even before the ocean pops up on the horizon, gentle country roads present an opportunity to observe wildlife (if you're patient) and see some pretty country side as you pedal past classic white New England churches, weathered stone walls, and open country fields.

The ride skirts the ocean along Seabrook. Seabrook is an old New Hampshire town where whaling boats were once built and residents were known for their Yorkshire accents. Today Seabrook is virtually a one-industry town, and the nuclear power plant, Seabrook Station, is located here and still is controversial today.

Seabrook is also home to the Science and Nature Center at Seabrook Station. The Center is a museum that uses audiovisual aids to illustrate energy, electricity, science, and wildlife. Aquariums and a touch pool are featured. Additionally bus tours visit the power plant site and the training center simulator, an exact replica of Seabrook Station's control room. The Owascoag Trail is a 0.7-mile self-guiding nature walk through a salt marsh and woods. A picnic area is also available. There is no charge for visiting. Call (800) 338-7482 in New England for hours of operation.

Hampton-Salisbury, MA.

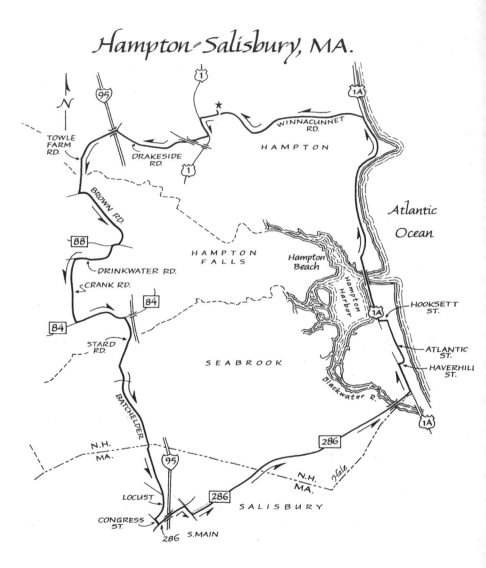

RIDE INFORMATION

Highlights: Pretty. Horse farms. Rock walls. Salt marsh offers wildlife sightings (Great Blue Herons, turtles, ducks, etc.). A long stretch of ocean views. Public beaches. Science and Nature Center at Seabrook Station.

Start: Begin at Hampton's Lane Library, at the corner of Winnacunnet Road and Academy Avenue. Winnacunnet Road is just off Route 1 by the Galley Hatch Restaurant.

RIDE DIRECTIONS

0.0 **Turn right on Winnacunnet Road.**

0.2 **At fork in road, bear left by Galley Hatch to stop sign, then left on Route 1/Lafayette Road.**

0.5 **Go right on Drakeside Road.**
At the 1.0 mile mark, a salt marsh offers lots of wildlife observation—Great Blue herons, turtles, mallard ducks—you just need the patience.

1.8 **At stop sign, turn left on Towle Farm Road (unmarked).**

3.0 **At stop sign/T-intersection, go left on Brown Road (unmarked).**

4.1 **At stop sign/T-intersection, go right on Route 88 (unmarked).**

4.2 **Go left on Drinkwater (by Hampton Falls Town Hall).**

4.8 **Left on Crank (unmarked, stone walls flank both sides of the road at this turn. Also a yellow farm house on left after turn.). This road becomes Garrison on the other end.**
The sun creates lacy patterns on the road as it shines through the tree canopy overhead.

5.7 **At stop sign/T-intersection, go left on Route 84 (unmarked).**

6.2 **Go right on Stard Road—just before bridge (unmarked. Road curves to left after you turn on it).**

7.2   At stop sign, continue straight—now on Batchelder (unmarked). The road becomes Locust.

9.4   At stop sign/T-intersection, go left on Congress Street (unmarked, Bartlett's Farm stand is here), then an almost immediate left at stop sign/T-intersection on Route 286E (unmarked).

9.9   At stop light, continue straight on Route 286E. Continue to follow signs for Route 286E.

11.3   Turn right on South Main.

12.8   At stop sign, turn right on 286E. A wide breakdown lane here.

Brown's Seafood is along this road. Excellent lunch spot.

13.7   At stop light, turn left on Route 1A.

14.1   Right on Haverhill to end of road, then a left on Atlantic.

14.7   At stop sign, turn left on Hooksett Road, then shortly (a block), take a right at stop light, on Route 1A.

Nice ocean views along here—once you're past the congested Hampton Beach area. Hampton Beach State Park is located at 15.6 miles.

Bathrooms are available at 16.5 miles—across from the Casino Ballroom.

18.0   Go left on Route 101E/Winnacunnett Road.

20.1   Back at Hampton's Lane Library on your right.

Doug French

About the Author

Linda Chestney began her cycling career on a red Schwinn with no gears, but on the flat plains of the Upper Midwest you don't need much more. Family and schooling eventually brought her to the East Coast. These days she tools around on a sleek, deep purple, metallic, 21-speed Terry.

In addition to writing several books on bicycling, Chestney writes feature articles and poetry for regional and national magazines on a variety of subjects, often on the topic of art. She has also worked as a public relations professional for more than twenty-five years.

She holds a degree in interior design from Chamberlayne (now Mount Ida) in Boston, a B.A. in psychology from Gordon College in Wenham, Massachusetts, where she also concentrated in journalism, and a master's degree in nonfiction writing from the University of New Hampshire.

A "newcomer" New Englander of thirty years, Chestney was originally a "flatlander" from South Dakota. She returns occasionally to the Midwest to see relatives, check out the cowboy boots, and bring back a tumbleweed or two. She resides on the Seacoast of New Hampshire with her husband and three pooches. Their house is tucked in the woods where deer and cross-country skiers roam.